"*Fierce Marriage* is the story of a couple learning and striving to put Christ above all else, in all matters of marriage. When two young authors get the roo surely trust the *fruit*."

Gary Thomas, bestselling auth

"Ryan and Selena are one of those coupl lived out day to day what they write about. *Fierce Marriage* is an incredible read that will inspire, encourage, and bring hope to your relationship."

Jefferson Bethke, *New York Times* bestselling author

"In *Fierce Marriage*, Ryan and Selena boldly open up about what they have faced in marriage, using their experiences to bring to light the biblical principles that should be the foundation for every marriage. Their vulnerability is captivating. Their marriage stories are familiar and relatable. Ryan and Selena passionately share God's truth about marriage, encouraging husbands and wives to pursue and fulfill their purpose of having a fierce marriage that points others to the heart of God."

Aaron and Jennifer Smith, founders
of HusbandRevolution.com
and UnveiledWife.com

"*Fierce Marriage* makes the case for having a covenant marriage and choosing to prayerfully and gracefully get through the 'yuck' of our own poor choices, whether in our attitudes or shortcomings. This book will help each spouse work toward becoming their best self in life and marriage. It shows spouses how each one can play a role in helping one another grow to their fullest potential, as iron sharpens iron. The Fredericks give practical applications that will help you keep God at the center of your marriage and life."

Fawn Weaver, founder of The Happy Wives Club

"Ryan and Selena are an inspiring example of what a fun, thriving, Christ-centered marriage can be! Our own marriage has been blessed because of their wisdom. This book will entertain you, challenge you, inspire you, and equip you with practical tools you can use to start building a stronger relationship with your spouse and a stronger relationship with God. *Fierce Marriage* will have a huge impact on your marriage!"

Dave and Ashley Willis, founders of StrongerMarriages
.com and authors of *7 Days to a Stronger Marriage*

"The challenges we face as married couples are fierce, so we must pursue each other with a radical love. Ryan and Selena Frederick know all about what that means, and their book *Fierce Marriage* challenges couples to love each other in the same way. With a perfect combination of a gospel-centered foundation, marital authenticity, and practical encouragement, *Fierce Marriage* will help any couple grow in their relationship as they're reminded of the high calling of marriage."

Scott Kedersha, director of marriage ministry,
Watermark Community Church

"I often hear people talk a lot but in the end don't end up really saying anything. We use a lot of words but end up skating around the topics most people want direct and clear insights and answers for. I have watched what Ryan and Selena have built with *Fierce Marriage* over the years and been impressed by their work. This book will give you direct and concrete solutions for your marriage, young or old."

Craig Gross, StrongerMarriages.com
and XXXchurch.com

"Ryan and Selena love each other, love marriage, and love Christ. Reading about that love as it pours out page after page is a huge encouragement to anyone looking to pursue their spouse the way Christ pursues us."

Adam Griffin, spiritual formation pastor,
The Village Church, Dallas, Texas

FIERCE
MARRIAGE

RADICALLY PURSUING
EACH OTHER IN LIGHT OF
CHRIST'S RELENTLESS LOVE

RYAN *AND* **SELENA FREDERICK**

BakerBooks
a division of Baker Publishing Group
Grand Rapids, Michigan

Published by Baker Books
a division of Baker Publishing Group
PO Box 6287, Grand Rapids, MI 49516-6287
www.bakerbooks.com

Printed in the United States of America

Library of Congress Cataloging-in-Publication Data
Names: Frederick, Ryan, 1983– author. | Frederick, Selena, 1982– author.
Title: Fierce marriage : radically pursuing each other in light of Christ's relentless love / Ryan and Selena Frederick.
Description: Grand Rapids : Baker Publishing Group, 2018. | Includes bibliographical references and index.
Identifiers: LCCN 2017051459 | ISBN 9780801075308 (pbk. : alk. paper)
Subjects: LCSH: Marriage—Religious aspects—Christianity.
Classification: LCC BV835 .F725 2018 | DDC 248.8/44—dc23
LC record available at https://lccn.loc.gov/2017051459

The authors are represented by Alive Literary Agency, 7680 Goddard Street, Suite 200, Colorado Springs, CO 80920, www.aliveliterary.com.

18 19 20 21 22 23 24   7 6 5 4 3 2

green
press
INITIATIVE

For Jesus, whose fierce, one-way love
is the only reason we're still married.

Contents

Foreword

Your marriage isn't about you.

It's not even about your marriage.

Ultimately, your marriage is about proclaiming the power and glory of Jesus Christ.

That's the foundation from which Ryan and Selena write *Fierce Marriage*. When discussing conflict, Selena wisely points out, "Jesus is not just a means to a better life; he *is* the better life. . . . Christ is every answer."

The problem for most of us is the bent of our lives. Christianity is an extreme religion, but we try to live it in the margins. Jesus said to love the Lord our God with *all* our heart, soul, mind, and strength, but we pass this off as hyperbole. We think, *Surely half is better than none.*

The Christian life is about becoming centered on God (Matt. 6:33). We seek to love with his love, think his thoughts, and live for his will. When a soul is surrendered to God, it is focused on worship and service. Love God and love others. Praise God and be devoted to good works (Titus 2:14). Those are the two hinges on which the Christian life turns.

A marriage crashes when we *stop* asking, "What does it mean to worship God in this situation?" and "What good works can I do in this situation?" and *start* asking, "How can I get my own way?"

The only "fix" is for one or both spouses to re-center their lives around worship of and service for God. If husband and wife wake up with a commitment to worship and serve, they will be delighted in their marriage. If only one spouse wakes up with a commitment to worship and serve, that's the spouse who will have the most joy in their marriage and be less vulnerable to disappointments within it.

Think of it this way: Has anyone ever lived with more peace, more joy, and more contentment than Jesus? Of course not. Yet his closest companions included a doubter, a couple of zealous hotheads, and a thief who became a traitor. None of their self-centeredness colored his days or his attitude, because Jesus lived a life of worship and service.

Fierce Marriage is the story of a couple learning and striving to put Christ above all else, in all matters of marriage. In the words of the Fredericks, "You don't fight for your marriage as much as Christ uses your marriage to fight for you. You don't pursue your spouse's heart as much as Christ uses your spouse to pursue your heart. You don't prize your spouse's affection with nearly the same ferocity with which Christ prizes yours. . . . That's the most exciting (albeit counterintuitive) aspect of marriage! It's not about you. It's all about Jesus. It always has been."

Gary Thomas
author of *Sacred Marriage* and *Cherish*

Introduction

This isn't your typical marriage book. At least we don't think it is. In our experience, there are many valuable resources about marriage, particularly in modern Christendom. We've observed that books in the Christian marriage category tend to fall on either side of what we call the hopeful-helpful intersection, which sometimes proves problematic. Here's what we mean.

Hopeful books offer what we need for eternal hope: reminders of the gospel, deep explorations of scriptural truth, and theologically rich prose. While these books are incredible, they can leave us wondering where we should go from there. Our hearts and heads are filled but our hands are left wondering what's next. The reader is charged with discovering the particulars of how to apply their newfound knowledge.

Helpful books are the inverse. They offer plenty of practical advice—action steps—without troubling too much with the underlying theological truths behind them. The tragedy with these books is that readers rarely learn the reasons behind the actions they take. We hear what to do without understanding why we are doing it—not truly, anyway. Our behavior changes for a time but our beliefs are largely unaffected. In our years of speaking with and ministering to married couples, this has proven troublesome.

We wanted to write a book that was different. If we were going to add another book to the Christian marriage book stockpile, we wanted it all. We wanted a book that infused readers with deep, beautiful, eternal gospel truth while equipping them with time-tested, wisdom-fueled advice for how to apply it. In short, we envisioned a book that could meet readers at the intersection of hopeful and helpful.

Fierce Marriage is our attempt at exactly that. It's our "marriage manifesto." Our modern tell-all. An exposé revealing all we believe marriage can be according to the Bible. We've done the exegesis of Scripture, read the commentaries, compiled the research, and done our absolute best to synthesize gospel-centered help that is rooted in the never-failing hope of Christ. We've worked hard to discern how much to expect from you, how much you should expect from us, and what you can expect to have once you finish this book.

We made a decision early on to expect much from you, dear reader. We expect that you want to know more than just a few new techniques for helping your marriage. We expect that you want to grow deeper in your understanding of Scripture and how it applies to your marriage. And we expect that you want to learn to trust Jesus more—with your heart, and with that of your spouse.

From us, you can expect our best work. You can expect honesty. We've shared stories in these pages that you will most likely never read elsewhere—they're the stories we'd share with you if we got dinner together. They're stories of pain, joy, romance, anger, and deep conviction. We've shared them all here, hopefully for your benefit. Finally, and most of all, you can expect from us a heavy reliance on Scripture and commitment to what it says.

Now, from this book you can expect order with a heavy dose of levity. The following words are a distillation of ideas that have been passed through layer after layer of theological and editorial oversight. We're not theologians in the scholarly sense, so we have asked smarter men and women than us to keep us in line. The end result, we hope, is a relevant interpretation of timeless marital truths rooted in Scripture. The chapters of this book are loosely but intentionally organized to be hopeful first and helpful second.

We will start by sharing a key event in our lives and marriage that has forever shaped us. Chapters 2, 3, and 4 unpack foundational, irreplaceable concepts for Christian marriage (the meanings of the gospel, covenant, and love). Chapters 5 through 9 build on those foundational, hope-filled principles to provide gospel-centered help in the key areas of marriage: priorities, communication, money, sex, and conflict. Finally, chapter 10 casts a vision for what can be had and extends an invitation to those who will have it.

While we don't know everything, we promise to share what we do know honestly. We're not counselors or ordained ministers, nor do we claim to have all the answers. All we have is Jesus and more than half our lives together, and all we can do is talk about what he's done. We do know one thing for sure: we wouldn't be married today if it wasn't for the loving kindness and infinite grace of Christ.

Finally, thank you. Thank you for inviting us into your life as you read this book. And thank you for allowing us to speak into your marriage, your most sacred and personal relationship.

We hope and pray that this book blesses you and your marriage for years to come.

Stay fierce,

Ryan and Selena

1

Our Swiss Adventure

The Early Years

Pain insists upon being attended to. God whispers
to us in our pleasures, speaks in our consciences,
but shouts in our pains. It is his megaphone to
rouse a deaf world.

C. S. Lewis

RYAN

Selena and I celebrated our second anniversary on a jumbo jet
somewhere over the Atlantic Ocean. By the time we boarded
that flight, we had already faced doubt, division, and financial ruin. And I had almost died. Seriously. Here's how it
happened.

We got married in early September just before our junior
year of college. Almost two years later and just a few weeks
before graduation, neither of us had strong career prospects.
I was a janitor for the mid-rise apartment building where we

lived (for the record, I preferred to be called a Master of the Custodial Arts). Selena worked as a barista at Starbucks.

Somewhere between studying for finals and procrastinating, Selena found a job opportunity on an equestrian recruitment website. She's always been passionate about horses—riding, jumping, grooming, and everything else.

When she discovered a job offer for an "au pair/groom" position at a private show-jumping facility near Zürich, Switzerland, it piqued her interest. She didn't think I'd go for it because the pay was totally unrealistic. However, when she half-jokingly proposed the opportunity, my response surprised her: "Let's do it!"

"Wait. What?" She was shocked.

"I'm serious, let's do it!"

That evening Selena emailed the person who posted the job, and in less than a week she was hired for the position. I was a "tagalong" hire who would perform random tasks around the equestrian facility. Together we would make two thousand Swiss francs per month, around eighteen hundred dollars at the time. It wasn't enough to live on, but we didn't care. We'd make it work.

After our college graduation ceremony, we were bursting with anticipation as we packed our bags, sold everything we could, and parked my bright yellow 1977 VW Bus in Selena's mom's garage. (I couldn't bring myself to sell it.) I'd miss her, but "The Twinkie" would have to wait there until we returned. Three days later we boarded a plane to spend a year in Europe.

There we were, a couple in our early twenties headed out for an adventure we'd never forget. We had seen the pictures of where we were going to work and live, and the facility looked like a dream—nestled in rural Switzerland with a breathtaking view of the Alps.

We had no clue that the adventure was doomed weeks before we boarded that first airplane.

Sabotaged by Sickness

My symptoms first became obvious on our layover in Copenhagen. I'd had a lingering cough for two months prior to our departure, but it was totally manageable until then. I assumed it was just allergies or, at worst, a mild case of bronchitis. Regardless, I'd been able to power through my shifts as a janitor, drink a few energy drinks, study all night, and go to class in the morning.

Sleep was truly an option during college, and one I'd opted out of far too many times. At one point during finals week I stayed up for three days straight in order to finish my capstone presentation. I faithfully lived my college-life motto: "When in doubt, caffeinate."

The long hours working and studying caught up with me in Europe. By the time we arrived at the Zürich airport, my body ached, I had constant chills, and nothing I did made me feel warmer. We both reasoned that I had a cold or viral sickness and it would pass in a few days. I figured it was my body detoxing from the long hours and horrible diet from the previous months (and by that I mean my whole college career).

Our new boss, Dani, met us at the baggage claim. We loaded our luggage into his car and headed off to his home—our workplace—in a small town about thirty minutes away. We would get settled, get acquainted, and within thirty-six hours, get to work. I informed Dani of my sickness and he agreed that I could take a few days off to feel better before starting my job.

As we discovered, the Swiss work ethic is just shy of super-human! Our work hours were 6:00 a.m. until well after 7:00 p.m., Monday through Saturday. At one point we calculated our hourly rate was around thirty cents per hour. Ridiculous, I know, but what an adventure!

Weeks passed, and instead of feeling better, I felt worse. Dani grew suspect of my sickness. He was a man of im-pressive stature, both physically and socially, and the closest thing to a real-life Terminator I've ever seen. He was six feet three inches tall, wore a tattered black leather jacket, spoke at least three languages, and had successfully built a small commercial empire through hard work and business acumen. He was a self-made man with a disdain for slackers.

Honestly, I don't blame him for his suspicion. We had been there for several weeks, and I had yet to work a full day. For all he knew, I was a "lazy American." I certainly felt that way. We had flown halfway around the world in pursuit of Selena's dream of riding horses in Europe, and I could hardly even get out of bed.

At the advice of a friend (and because we didn't want to pay full price for medicine), we had purchased traveler's insurance for thirty-five dollars per month. It wasn't in the budget, but we thought it would be a good investment. We decided it was time to use it. With some translation help from Dani, I scheduled an appointment for the next day with a small doctor's office a few kilometers away.

We didn't know what was wrong, and as it turned out, the doctors didn't know either. My doctor did the best he could with the equipment he had on-site. He deduced that I had an aggressive bacterial infection that was best treated by antibiotics, pain medicine, and rest. He prescribed the appropriate medications and told me to call back in a week.

I left, made a beeline to the closest pharmacy, and swallowed those pills as quickly as I could. The medicine helped! Finally I felt better and my energy was restored. I carried on with my tasks as a farmhand: shoveling dung, building and repairing barns, and anything else Dani assigned. I didn't enjoy the job, per se, but getting fresh air felt incredible.

My enthusiasm didn't last long though. While the pain medication made me feel better, the antibiotics weren't curing me. My symptoms subsided while the problem—whatever it was—grew worse. Nonetheless, I pushed through. I worked every day until my strength was gone.

Every morning I woke up, popped a painkiller, took my amoxicillin, and started work. By noon my body was throbbing and weak. So I'd take a thirty-minute power nap, down another painkiller, and get out to the barn. Sometimes I'd finish the entire day; other times I was too weak to continue. Eventually I became incapable of working as the sickness overwhelmed my body.

One morning, Dani called a meeting with us and his wife, Sabine. It didn't take long to realize where the conversation was going. Dani and Sabine were unsatisfied with our performance. Though Selena worked very hard, Dani said she only completed the tasks of "one third of a person." They had hired two workers and, in their minds, we equaled less than one. I was nearly useless with some unidentified sickness and Selena, though well intentioned, was ill-suited for the job. (To be honest, there were some dynamics going on with other workers at the facility that may have influenced their perception. But it's not worth getting into. Besides, perception is reality, right?)

I felt helpless. I understood Dani's frustration with my output, but I was powerless to do anything about it. Was I the reason our dream—Selena's dream—would end here? Was I the reason for our failure?

To make matters worse, we were supposed to teach their five-year-old daughter English in our off time. She was very shy and hardly warmed up to either of us. We managed to teach her ten words. Dani and Sabine added that to the pile of failed expectations.

After twenty minutes of hearing their disappointment, we settled on an arrangement. We had two weeks to prove we were worth keeping around. Otherwise we were fired and had to return to the States.

Disaster Deepens

Selena and I spent the evening discussing possible ways to work harder and faster. What if we woke up earlier and slept less? How about sweeping and mucking stalls in a new pattern to reduce the time required? It took a few hours to get there, but eventually we resigned all hope of staying.

Any pace increase would be unsustainable and the pay wasn't worth it. We could barely afford groceries, let alone travel throughout Europe. Even if we could, we wouldn't get far with one day off each week. Also our student loans, although deferred, would be knocking on our financial door soon, so any money we might have "saved" was already spoken for.

Reality is such a buzzkill.

After about two hours of deliberating, we decided to propose a new plan to Dani and Sabine. We would spend the next two weeks working our tails off, then we'd pack our nonessentials into their plastic crates and toss them in their basement before hopping on a train to explore Europe for two to three weeks. We had no clue how we'd pay for the trip, but that wasn't important. I started planning our trip on an Excel spreadsheet, meticulously mapping the days, train times, and hostel options one by one.

We were literally going for broke. Our original plan had failed, but at least we'd go out in a blaze of glory!

The next morning we spoke with Dani and told him our idea. He agreed to let us store our stuff at their place. I could tell he was relieved to end our arrangement.

I may have been short on strength but I still had plenty of pride. I wanted to prove to Dani that I wasn't lazy—that he had made a huge mistake doubting the Fredericks. I wanted him to wish we would stay.

We returned to our jobs with refreshed vigor. My final task was a big one: I had to remove, level, and rebuild the floors of four horse stalls. It may not sound like much, but for one guy who had never done anything like it, it would take all of two weeks. I was determined to get it done. I had to convince myself—and Selena, I thought—that I wasn't the reason we couldn't cut it.

I started by prying up the old rubber mats that lined the floors of each stall. The smell of horse urine was so strong I had to hold my breath while pulling each two-foot by two-foot square up to set it aside.

The next step was to level the floor, which was now a sloppy, muddy, pee-soaked mess. Dani had a pile of gravel

21

delivered and waiting nearby. I shoveled the material into a wheelbarrow, dumped multiple loads in each stall, and compacted the new base with the underside of the shovel. After some fine adjustments the foundation was ready. All of this took about three days, and I went to bed exhausted each night.

My next task was to place twelve-inch hexagon paver bricks on the gravel to create solid flooring for the horses. The bricks had been delivered fifty feet away from the project site. I got to work loading them into the wheelbarrow and carting them across the rugged terrain to my site. The labor was tough, but with my mysterious sickness it seemed impossible.

Surely I'd start feeling better soon. I just had to work harder. I had to prove I wasn't the reason for our dream's demise.

Again I pressed on with the help of my pain meds. The only problem was that my antibiotic medication ran out on Friday and my doctor's office was closed on the weekends. So I doubled down on the painkillers and finished Saturday's work the best I could.

Throughout the whole ordeal, I experienced wild swings of hot and cold flashes. One moment I'd be shivering so violently from chills that I needed to soak in a blazing-hot bath. The next moment I'd be so hot I would drip sweat like I was in a military-style CrossFit class. The Sunday my pain meds ran out was the worst yet. The hot/cold cycles were amplified and there was no chance I'd work the next morning. I told Dani I needed to rest and mentioned I should go into town to see my doctor and refill my prescription. He informed me that it was Swiss National Day and no businesses were open. I was out of luck.

I spent Monday trying to rest, except I was feeling worse than ever. Selena and I started to worry. Whatever this sickness was, it was accelerating and there was nowhere to go and nobody who could help. I hunkered down for the evening and decided to call my doctor as soon as his office opened.

The next morning was much chillier than usual, and it had started to rain. I immediately called my doctor's office once business hours resumed, but no one picked up. I asked Dani if he could give me a ride; he was apologetic but unavailable. I asked to borrow the bicycle, but Sabine had taken it for the day. My only option was to walk the four kilometers by myself in the rain.

I couldn't take another day of this, so I headed out on foot.

The Awful Truth

About forty minutes later I arrived in the lobby of my doctor's office. Usually I would practice my German as I spoke with the receptionist and nurses. Today was different; I had nothing German to say. Thankfully most Swiss people speak English pretty well.

"I need help, now!" I said with urgency and an elevated volume.

"But you don't have an appointment," the receptionist replied, a little puzzled.

I'm sure I was a sad sight to behold: shivering out of control, soaked from head to toe, and the color of my face matching the stark white on the walls.

"I don't care, I need to see a doctor now," I insisted.

"Well, your doctor is on holiday for Swiss National Day and won't return for another week," she said.

Not only had my prescription run out on Friday after-noon but my doctor's office was closed Saturday, Sunday, and Monday—and now he would be gone for an entire week. I honestly didn't think I'd survive that long.

"Please help me," I said, as I shuddered.

The receptionist had mercy. She instructed me to sit in the lobby so she could assess the situation.

After a few minutes a nurse invited me back to a part of the clinic I had never seen before. She ran the routine tests I'd grown accustomed to: check the pulse (always fast), take the temperature (always hot), prick the finger to test the blood (still infected). Nothing new.

What was new, however, was the profuse sweating, shak-ing, and elevated panic I was experiencing.

By that time she sensed something was very wrong. She asked me to wait a few more minutes so she could speak with the other doctor and bring him up to speed on my case.

I needed to lie down. I was seated on a metal table about the length of my body so I swiveled around, put my feet up, and lay back. It felt good to rest after walking all that way in the rain. However, by then I was shaking so violently that it was a fight to stay on the table. I barely managed not to fall off.

Finally the other doctor entered the room.

"Please sit up," he said with Swiss efficiency.

I obliged.

He pressed an icy stethoscope to my chest and listened. He moved it and listened some more, now with a concerned look on his face.

He pulled the earpieces from his ears, pushed his glasses back into place on the bridge of his nose, and glanced through my medical chart again. Then he paused.

Again with the stethoscope. This time he didn't move it at all; he just kept it positioned in the same place. After two minutes of listening, he pulled the earpieces out again and stepped back.

"We need to get you to the hospital right away," he said.

I immediately thought of our meager pay and limited insurance. "How much is that going to cost?"

He responded with something I'll never forget.

"You either go to the hospital or you die. You choose. Something is terribly wrong with your heart." I immediately thought of Selena.

SELENA

Ryan had been gone for over an hour, but I didn't think anything of it. Rain was pouring down, and I had just finished exercising one of the younger horses. Wet, muddy, and a bit frustrated from the past week's events, I was more than ready to get the horses put away and start their lunch so I could get my own and take a nap.

"Selena?" Dani called for me in the barn.

"Yes, in here," I hollered back while brushing down the fidgety young horse.

"We need to go to the hospital. A doctor called us. They said Ryan is sick and we need to go." The anxiety in his voice made my heart skip a beat.

"Okay, I'll be there in a sec . . ."

"We need to go now," Dani said more forcefully. "The other groom will finish here."

I left immediately with Dani—with stained breeches, muddy boots, a damp sweatshirt, and my wallet. Off we went to the local hospital.

I remember thinking, *I hope he's okay. I wonder why we all need to go down there. Maybe he's too tired to walk back and it's really rainy.* I had no idea what to expect.

Growing up with a mom who is a registered nurse showed me how to keep a level head when sickness or injury happened in our family. My worry level for Ryan's health was about a three on a scale of ten. Being the young wife and naïve twenty-three-year-old that I was, I figured Ryan and I would have plenty of time to chat and process the day's events back at our little apartment on the farm that evening (antibiotics in hand, of course).

After arriving at the hospital, Dani and I walked into the room where Ryan was sitting up in a bed. The doctor came in and explained that they were going to do an ultrasound of his heart (an echocardiogram) because they had heard a murmur during their examination.

The severity of the situation started to sink in after the technician gave us the results of the ultrasound. Ryan had a bacterial growth, approximately two centimeters long, attached to his mitral valve. Every time his heart beat, and the valve opened and closed, the growth would flap around like a flag. That was the murmur they heard.

"Okay, so how do we treat this?" I asked with fear in my voice. "What do we do?"

After the technician explained the ultrasound results, the doctor said that we needed to go now to the main hospital in Zürich via ambulance so the staff there could monitor Ryan. They had called to consult the head of cardiology at the state hospital in Zürich, and his orders were to get Ryan there as quickly as possible.

Pushed to My Limit

We were escorted to an ambulance. Ryan was wheeled in a hospital bed while hooked up to a heart monitor. I walked alongside him in my muddy attire. I had nothing but a few Swiss francs in my wallet, my passport, a nearly empty international calling card, and a rail pass. More importantly, I had no idea where we were going, how or when we'd get back, or if Ryan would be alive for the next week.

I felt numb to the situation. Neither of us could process exactly what was happening, and as we sat in the back of the ambulance with few private moments to ourselves, shame set in.

What did I say to my husband, who had given so much for me? Out of my own selfishness, I had allowed frustration and bitterness to build up in my heart. I had let myself grow angry at him because of a situation—a sickness—that was out of his control.

How and where did I begin?

I thought, *I'm sorry for being so frustrated with you for being sick the last few weeks. I'm sorry for trying to push you to work a little harder and a little longer so we could stay in Switzerland in pursuit of my riding dream. I'm sorry that I am a horrible and selfish wife. I'm sorry that I had no idea that my pushing you was almost killing you.*

All I wanted to do was apologize. There were no tears or other emotions yet.

We arrived at Triemli Hospital, where the Swiss head of cardiology was waiting to examine Ryan. After a long afternoon of tests, fear and frustration started to set in. I felt like paperwork and bills were already piling up and we had no money to pay them. With everything being written and spoken in Swiss-German, it took us twice as long to communicate with hospital staff and insurance people.

I spent the night holding his hand and sleeping in a chair next to his bed. I was still in my dried, muddy riding clothes, and Ryan was finally experiencing some comfort—a sweet relief for both of us.

The doctors didn't know what type of bacteria the growth was. So the plan of choice was to administer a cocktail of antibiotics intravenously for a week in hopes of killing the infection.

We were looking at being in the hospital for at least a week. That meant I needed to figure out how to get back to the farm to get everything we needed.

Smartphones weren't a thing yet, so I had to find my way back the old-fashioned way: ask someone for directions and write them down with pen and paper. I needed familiarity, I needed to get back to the only place we knew as "home," and I needed some time alone.

Through broken English, a kind nurse talked me through the best route home. He spoke, I wrote. His directions guided me to navigate to the trolley, through the main train station to the correct train, and eventually to my stop. I kissed Ryan goodbye and assured him that I would be back the next day.

I set out alone back to the farm. As I rode the trolley and trains, fear began to grip my heart and mind. I was alone in a foreign country, and my husband—my best friend—was helpless in the hospital. We had little money to our name, and I was in the same stinky clothes I had worn for the past two days.

Finally I made it back to the farm. Upon my arrival I received a stern reprimand from Sabine for not doing the laundry correctly. Another failure.

I couldn't take any more. I broke down and cried. I cried because I was afraid. I cried because I was angry at myself and furious at God. I relentlessly asked him, "Why! Why Ryan? Why now? What did we do to deserve this?"

No answer, only more tears.

The reality of the situation sank in as the shock wore off. Ryan was dangerously sick and at death's doorstep. Death. I had finally reached the end of my already-frayed rope. I got down on my knees and opened my clenched fists that I had been shaking at God. Then I raised my hands in surrender and humbly pleaded with him to help me. To help us.

At that moment, his peace flooded my soul.

Even though I had no idea what the coming days would bring, I knew God was with me. He was there with us, and his presence was all we needed.

A Life-or-Death Gamble

Within days Ryan's parents had arrived in Zürich and were at the hospital with us. We were both deeply relieved and thankful for their presence and support.

After a week in the hospital with Ryan on intravenous antibiotics, the doctors performed another ultrasound to measure the size of the bacterial growth. If it was smaller, we'd have tangible hope. If it didn't shrink, Ryan would have to undergo one of the most invasive surgeries a human can face, with a real chance of not making it out alive.

The test results confirmed our fears. Despite the treatment, the bacteria had actually grown. The doctors needed to open him up and remove it as soon as possible or risk it breaking off, flowing to his brain, and causing a stroke.

They put Ryan on the schedule for open-heart surgery the next morning.

Ryan was twenty-two years old, and he'd always been concerned with his legacy. He'd always wanted to make a lasting mark on the world, even if he wouldn't be here to see it made. So he took to his journal and began to write.

As surgery approached, Ryan wrote his will. He wrote last letters to his parents, his brother, a few best friends, and me. After he finished, he closed his journal and we began to talk—just us.

We talked about our future and the babies we would have if he survived. We discussed the reality of my life if he didn't make it—how he didn't want me to be alone, how he wanted to make sure I was cared for in his absence. Needless to say, it was an emotional conversation.

He spent the last part of the evening watching Swiss TV and chatting with his dad before we all returned to our own beds, anxious for the morning.

The next day we woke and went to the hospital. They let me walk alongside Ryan to where they would prep him for surgery. We held each other in a long hug, kissed goodbye, and said, "See you in a few hours."

After the four longest hours of my life, the doctor finally called us over.

"We removed the bacterial growth," he said, "and did not have to use a prosthetic valve. He has a bit of backflow, but it is manageable. And since we kept his valve, he won't have to be on blood-thinning medicine the rest of his life. He's in recovery right now, and we will let you see him after he's moved to the ICU."

Praise God! He'd made it! In a moment, with a few sentences, we had our future back. Our dreams of life together, babies, and memories would still happen. I still had my husband.

After a few minutes they informed us that Ryan had been moved. I followed the nurse down the corridor, through the heavy doors, and around the curtain to where Ryan was resting. I raced over to kiss him on the forehead. He was still on the ventilator, and countless other machines were beeping, flashing, and pulsing. It was a difficult sight to see, but my husband was still alive.

After a few hours the doctors gave the go-ahead to remove the ventilator. Once it was removed, he began to wake up. The doctors and nurses were gathered around with Ryan's parents and me.

Disoriented, he asked, "Is it over? Is it over?"

"Yes, babe! You made it!" I replied. "The surgery is over!"

He opened his eyes and with a groggy voice exclaimed, "We can have babies!"

Giggling, I replied, "Yes! Lots!"

He recognized my voice and became more aware of the situation.

"No . . . ," he said with a drowsy sigh.

We all had a good laugh.

I was relieved, to say the least. My Ryan was here, alive. Soon he would be on the mend.

2

Matters of the Heart

How the Gospel Revolutionizes Marriage

Redemption is not perfection. The redeemed must
realize their imperfections.

John Piper

RYAN

I will never forget the feeling of relief when I cracked my eyes
open after surgery to see Selena standing by my side. Just
hours before we had been crying and wondering if we'd share
another day. We'd wondered if we'd get to raise children,
make more memories, or have the simplest conversations
again. Nothing was guaranteed. Everything was at risk and
would be lost should I not wake up again.

When I awoke, those fears vanished in an instant with the
good news that I was still alive. That moment has shaped

our marriage in the years since, and it has forever changed the way we feel compelled to love each other.

Not every couple has the opportunity (if you'd call it that) to confront life's fragility so early in their marriage. But it highlighted for us what I believe we all want to feel in our relationships—that love is precious, that our spouses are absolute gifts, that life together is a blessing beyond measure. When there was a chance I could lose my life, I instantly felt the possible grief of losing Selena too. That one experience put the value of love into stark focus for us. I think it's because we're wired to need and cherish real love. We all deeply desire to love and be loved unconditionally and without expiration. Yet that particular brand of love has become harder and harder to find.

Elusive Love

Trisha wrote to us through the Fierce Marriage website and described how she experienced a long trail of broken dating relationships. But she had finally met a guy who captured her heart. He was close to proposing, and she was getting nervous. "What if something is wrong with me?" she asked. "What if I'm not capable of loving another person for the rest of my life?" Trisha asked us whether love was something she could learn with the right actions, thoughts, and habits, or if her latest relationship was doomed to end the same way the others had.

Craig emailed me when he felt like he had messed up for the last time. His addiction to pornography was destroying his marriage and devastating his wife. They had been to counseling and they were seeking help from pastors, but he failed over and over again. He thought for sure that his wife's love would run out—that her patience would expire. He agonized about whether his behavior would make him unlovable to his wife and if they'd ever work through his addiction together.

Countless individuals have sent us messages because their spouses have told them that they've fallen out of love. I'm reminded of Zach, who no matter how hard he tried could not convince his wife to honor their marriage. She had emotionally detached and bought the lie that their love had been "lost" forever. Her feelings had changed, so she decided to move on. Zach could do nothing. He blamed himself for losing her love and wondered what he could have done differently. I doubt it was entirely his fault. Now he wonders if love can ever be found and if it's worth risking again.

Julie wrote us because she felt that she'd never find true love, that "the one" she was destined to marry would never even know she existed. She desperately wanted to find a man she could call her own. She wanted to feel complete, and only having a husband could accomplish that—or so she thought. Her anxiety multiplied as each one of her friends married and eventually started having kids. She'd soon be the only unmarried, childless person in her friend group, and it was tearing her apart. Where is love for Julie? Where is her hope?

If you've ever had questions or doubts like these people, you're not alone! We have yet to meet *anyone* who feels like they've got this whole love thing on lockdown. Everyone doubts. Everyone feels inadequate to some degree. You know why? Because we are! You, me, everybody. We all have gaps in our ability to give and receive love. On our own, we're all missing something.

Entire industries exist around the idea of love—defining it, finding it, expressing it, feeling it, and understanding it. It makes sense, when you think about it. We're buying what they're selling—in bulk! We'll try anything if it promises to bring us closer to true love and authentically connecting with another person. Dress right, eat right, act right, speak right, impress the right person, and then you'll have love—you'll *be* loved.

The problem is that nothing works. At least not forever.

It's just like the painkillers and amoxicillin I received from my Swiss doctor before my diagnosis. Our effort helps us feel better for a short time, but the sickness remains. We have this nuisance of our own humanity and that of others. We must face—and defeat—the problem of sin if we're ever going to experience true love. We need a deeper cure than anything we can find in this world. We need to be healed from the inside out. Everything else is a distraction. We've been taking painkillers but what we desperately need are the hands of a skilled heart surgeon.

In other words, we need Jesus.

The Gospel Changes Everything in Marriage

Growing up in a port city, I often sat with my dad and watched as massive cargo ships came and went from the bay. The maritime monstrosities crept through the water into port, each vessel laden with thousands of containers full of countless treasures. The ships were so heavy they had to shut off their engines more than a mile out just to slow down to a manageable speed prior to docking. It was the captain's job to skillfully maneuver around land masses (above and below water) and aim their bow perfectly to get within tugboat range. If at any point they lost control, disaster was imminent—the ship's mass and momentum were too great to redirect its course or stop it by external means.

Marriage is like a cargo ship. It's massive, packed with value, and more powerful than we could ever comprehend. And like a ship without a rudder, a marriage without the gospel will careen out of control.

But the gospel is a capable rudder for an idea as weighty as marriage. It's only through Christ that we are able to understand unconditional love, feel the full weight and joy of covenant, and experience firsthand the radical grace and forgiveness necessary for loving one another until death.

However, do we all agree on what the gospel actually is? Let's take a (very) quick detour to make sure. I promise the clarity is well worth it.

What Is Meant by "the Gospel"?

The gospel is the good news of God's grace for a sinful world. It is the grand story of creation, the fall, humankind's redemption, and our ultimate salvation through the life, death, resurrection, and ascension of Jesus Christ. There is no other way and no other name by which humans can be saved except by grace, through faith, in Christ.

John Piper said it like this: "The Gospel is the news that Jesus Christ, the Righteous One, died for our sins and rose again, eternally triumphant over all his enemies, so that there is now no condemnation for those who believe, but only everlasting joy."[1]

Before we move on I'd like to pause on the word *news*. The gospel is *not* good advice! Nor is it merely a collection of good teachings given by a good man somewhere in the Middle East a few thousand years ago. When we talk about the gospel being good *news* we're emphasizing the finished work of Christ—God in the flesh—on the cross for our salvation once and for all. It's finished, accomplished, done, complete, final. The gospel is a report of an event that has already happened and which bears real and eternal weight on life today.

That is the gospel, and there's nothing like it.

Now that we're all on the same page of what the gospel is, let's explore three massive ways it revolutionizes marriage: as our diagnosis, our cure, and our recovery.

Our Diagnosis: the Gospel Is Realistic about What to Expect

It's easy, in our culture, to idealize marriage. This is especially true for younger generations who have grown up seeing reality through the lens of social media. Authenticity is applauded and sharing your real life is celebrated—just as long as it's not *too* authentic or *too* real.

I once counseled a couple who met on a popular photo-sharing app. Months into their marriage he was already looking to run—completely panicked. "She's crazy!" he told me. But he wasn't innocent; she had complaints of her own. "He's untrustworthy and prideful!" she insisted. Neither person turned out to be who the other expected them to be. Their individual selfishness constantly clashed and created chaos in every area of their marriage.

I didn't know what to tell them. They married each other and committed to spending their lives—their *real, authentic* lives—with each other through better and worse. I think they were expecting a share-worthy marriage but what they got was a little too real—a little *too authentic*. I could only reply, "What exactly did you expect *worse* to look like?"

It's uncanny how many couples we meet who are shocked when they experience true difficulty in their marriage for the first time. I'm not talking about bickering about which direction the toilet paper should unroll or how to correctly squeeze the toothpaste. I'm talking about rubber-meets-the-road difficulty—the kind where both spouses wonder what they got themselves into and how they can get out. I'm talking about the kind of difficulty where sin actually *looks like sin*: unattractive, destructive, and dark.

The gospel revolutionizes marriage because in it, Jesus addresses sin for what it truly is and lovingly calls us to admit that we're sinners who desperately need his help. Jesus is God's love made flesh, but his love always goes hand-in-hand with calling would-be disciples to repentance. Calling us to repent is the most loving thing God can do. Anything less is an incomplete gospel and is idealistic, false, and bound to disappoint.

Of course, God makes every person in his image and endows them with intrinsic value, worth, and importance. He is a master craftsman and never makes mistakes! However, since the fall, recorded in Genesis 3, sin has contaminated every aspect of creation—your marriage included.

A husband and wife in a gospel-centered marriage will never expect each other to be perfect. Instead, they fully expect to fall short and always trust that Jesus is more than enough to meet their every need (2 Pet. 1:3). They will also expect to experience repentance regularly from both sides of the equation. That's the beauty of grace-fueled sanctification within the safety of covenant marriage—both spouses see their imperfection while valuing repentance as the character-refining work of the Holy Spirit.

Our Cure: the Gospel Transforms How We Love

I can't describe the sense of relief and joy I felt when I woke from surgery to hear Selena's voice. It's unexplainable. One moment I was sick and dying and the next I had received the cure. Everything I thought I had lost had suddenly been regained. Facing death has a way of magnifying life's preciousness. The worse the bad news is, the better the good news feels.

Just as a complete gospel diagnoses the sickness, it also administers the cure. The gospel revolutionizes marriage by showing us what to realistically expect from each other, but it doesn't leave us there—it also carries us forward! God rescues us from death, sets our feet on solid ground, and shows us a better way to love (1 Cor. 12:31).

The experience of God's love in Christ forever changes how you love each other—in three tangible ways. First, Jesus shows us that real love is vastly more powerful, costly, and rewarding than anything offered by the world. Our human definition of love pales in comparison to God's. The gospel shows us God's incomparable love, empowers us to love in a similar way, and assures us that loving each other according to God's design won't always be easy but *is* always worth it. We'll discuss this more in chapter 4.

Next, the gospel shows us exactly what *covenant* means and what we can expect to accomplish when we submit ourselves to loving each other within covenantal boundaries. We'll explore this more in chapter 3, but for now just imagine how your marriage would be if both of you based your choice to love not on the other person's performance but on the promises you have made.

Finally, experiencing the gospel transforms how you love by flooding your heart with grace, empathy, patience, and the capacity to forgive. For example, in my senior year of high school I job-shadowed a cardiothoracic surgeon for a week. During that time, I observed hours of open-heart surgery. I could never relate to the fear and pain the patients felt—until four years later when I received a heart surgery of my own. I now relish every opportunity I get to exchange recovery stories with fellow surgery recipients. I now have empathy.

The experience of radical grace multiplies the grace you feel for others—especially your spouse. You're compelled to love your spouse radically because of the radical love you've been given. You've been under Grace's knife; you know how the surgery feels. You've experienced for yourself what it's like to need Christ's righteousness to replace your own. And you now count your forgiveness as a priceless gift. The greater your experience of grace, the larger your capacity to give it. If "he who is forgiven little, loves little" (Luke 7:47), then it follows that the opposite is also true: he who is forgiven much, loves much. Prior to experiencing forgiveness, one might say, "How dare they sin against me?" But after sitting at death's door and being rescued from its hold, one would rather say, "How can I possibly hold their sin against them?" This shift in heart orientation brought on by the gospel forever changes how you love each other in marriage.

The gospel transforms our love in more ways than the above—as we will explore later. For now, suffice it to say that a gospel-centered marriage will have an otherworldly view of love as a result of experiencing the transformational love of God in Christ.

Our Recovery: the Gospel Provides Context for Real Married Life

The final way that the gospel revolutionizes marriage is by endowing us with eternal purpose. First, every happy and enjoyable moment in your life together is amplified in light of God's never-ending goodness and grace. Every good thing is infinitely better when the glory goes to God—which is creation's purpose—and the same is certainly true of marriage!

Also, so much of life can feel like a daily grind. For every marriage mountaintop, there are dozens of valleys and hundreds of miles of meandering trail somewhere in the foothills. The gospel is the compass that keeps our marriage on a steady course through the fiercest storms, the most monotonous lulls, and the trickiest traverses.

Selena and I have said it many times: if it wasn't for Jesus, we would have been divorced years ago. Why would we say that? Because at times giving up would have been so easy—or so we felt.

Without the call to covenant, we could never have worked through communication issues that seemed to last forever. Without the experience of grace, Selena could never have forgiven me for sinning against her. And without God's clear definition of love, I could have easily justified walking away the moment my feelings urged me toward the door.

Even more than the strength to endure difficulty, the gospel affords us unmatched joy while doing so! How? Because our hope is eternal and this story we're part of is not about us. It's about Jesus. Every aspect of your marriage is designed by God for his eternal glory and your ultimate joy. Through the gospel—the good news that Christ saves—your marriage has infinite power and purpose because it points to an infinite, powerful God.

Every time you love your spouse when it's hard, you reflect the unrelenting love of God in Christ. Every time you uphold your covenant despite wanting to give up, you mirror God's unfailing promise to redeem his people. And every time you enjoy oneness and unity in intimacy, you foreshadow the unity and oneness that God's people—the Bride—will experience with Jesus—the Bridegroom—in heaven.

That is why we'll continue to sound the trumpet of the gospel for marriage. Only in the gospel do you have purpose beyond now, beyond you, and beyond measure. In Christ alone, by grace alone, and through faith alone, you have access to the infinite goodness of the eternal God both in this life and the next. Everything about marriage points to the gospel, and by God's grace your marriage can do the same.

Transformed Heart, Transformed Marriage

In his book *Sacred Marriage*, Gary Thomas asked one of the most stunning questions of our married lives: "What if God designed marriage to make us holy more than to make us happy?"[2]

This single idea flips the modern concept of marriage on its head. It changes how you view yourself, your spouse, and your covenant. More importantly, the view that marriage is all about Jesus—your holiness in light of the gospel—is the single belief that will maximize the total love and enjoyment you will experience in your union. God's goal in your marriage is to reveal his unconditional love as you learn what it truly means to love another in his or her imperfection.

Christ is our ultimate goal, and the bounty of a life lived in full light of the gospel includes everything else he promises: hope, peace, joy, and, most of all, love. As C. S. Lewis says, "But look for Christ and you will find Him, and with Him everything else thrown in."[3] Jesus isn't merely a means to a better marriage; your marriage is a means to better relationship with Jesus.

As I mentioned above, his work on the cross is more than an offer of good advice for living a more virtuous life (though a more virtuous life will be a result). It is a proclamation of good news about a work already finished. The distinction seems subtle, but it changes everything.

It leads us to ask the questions of *who* and *why* before asking *how* and *what*.

- Who is Christ? Who exactly does he say you are? Who does he say your spouse is?
- Why did God design marriage the way he did? Why did he send Christ to the cross? Why are you inclined to behave the way you do?

From there, we can address the practical "how" questions more effectively.

- How can I love an imperfect person unconditionally?
- How can I communicate more effectively—more lovingly?
- How can we overcome adversity that seems devastating?
- How can we gain agreement about money?

- How can we have a more fulfilling sex life?
- How can we stop fighting so often?

Don't worry; we'll discuss and answer those questions in due time. For now, we must remember that the gospel is not a recipe for behavior modification. The gospel changes hearts. When the good news of Christ changes our hearts, identity, and beliefs at their cores, behavioral change will follow for a lifetime.

Real change always starts in the heart. Always. And Christ is the only surgeon qualified to operate.

Marriage: a Journey of Redemption

After my surgery, I dreaded every ultrasound appointment. I feared the doctors would find something else wrong with my heart. The pain of recovery was too intense—I couldn't imagine having to start the whole process all over again. I would rather they didn't look at my heart at all. It was easier to ignore it and pretend I was healthy.

Maybe you feel the same way as you read this?

Is it unsettling to go to the doctor's office and let them poke around? Yes.

Are we reluctant to return for a checkup for fear of exposing another sickness? Definitely.

It's scary to be opened up—to be seen for who you are with all your faults, flaws, and failures. But that's exactly how Jesus loves you: for who you are. That's the person he died for. You. It's the same for your spouse, and God saw it good in his infinite wisdom to pair you together for the journey of redemption. The ultimate goal of this journey is the transformation of your heart into one that mirrors Jesus. However, there's a passage in the Bible that says, "In this world you will have trouble" (John 16:33 NIV). Our marriages are not spared from this reality.

In our time writing about marriage, we have encountered tens of thousands of people committed to strengthening their marriages through the truth of the gospel. Along the way, we have seen that there are common issues—you could almost say universal issues—that creep up in every marriage. Even godly marriages centered on God's truth and reliant on his strength aren't immune. In our marriages, we will have trouble. But take heart! Just as Jesus has overcome the world, there is a path to overcoming marriage obstacles God's way.

In the pages ahead, we want to show you how to fight fiercely for your marriage, see how your relationship mirrors God's love for his people, and learn from Jesus's sacrificial love. We want you to see how to build healthy boundaries with technology and gain the essential tools for healthy communication, sex, and personal finances. We also want to show you—and this is so inspiring for us—how your marriage fits into a larger plan for the kingdom of God.

If your marriage is meant for more than your happiness, then what is it meant for? We believe it is one of the primary avenues by which God will use you to make his name known to the ends of the earth. Wow! That's why we take marriage so seriously. That's why we're so committed to a right understanding of this covenant God established. That's why we want a fierce marriage. And we want you to have it too. There is so much joy to be experienced, and there is much at stake, so we better get going.

Father, you are good. You are infinitely more wonderful than anything we can imagine. Thank you for your grace over our lives and the lives of our readers. Thank you for revealing your Word to us through Scripture and through your Son, Jesus. We ask that you open our hearts, by your grace, to receive the exact wisdom we need to hear. Help us believe more fully in your gospel and understand the depths of your grace. Guide and instruct us, lead and convict us. And may our lives and marriages be walking, breathing accounts of your goodness, grace, and mercy in our lives. You deserve all honor and glory. In Jesus's name, Amen.

FOR REFLECTION

- On a scale of 0 to 10, how much is Jesus / the gospel involved in your marriage?

0	1	2	3	4	5	6	7	8	9	10
Not at all									Jesus is the center	

Why did you choose the number you did?

- How have you tried to improve your marriage in the past?
- Would you say these improvements were a head response (items checked off on a list) or a heart response (transformed by God; lasting change)?
- How long did the improvements last? Why do you think that is?

3

The Magnitude of Covenant

The Power and Purpose of Lifelong Commitment

> You don't really need to make a vow to stick with
> someone in the best of times. The inclination
> to run doesn't exist then. It's the low times the
> covenant is made for.
>
> Matt Chandler

SELENA

Ryan and I love visiting the coast. There's one memorable
spot on the Washington coast called Washaway Beach. More
formally known as North Cove, this beach is one of the
fastest eroding places in our hemisphere. It loses about a
hundred and fifty feet per year, and potentially more during
a harsh winter. The ocean has claimed much of the land
that was once there. It was intended to be a destination spot
for travelers, but anything built on or near it has literally
washed into the ocean! Washaway Beach is a dichotomy of

both beauty and destruction. It offers no permanence to its occupants. Numerous studies and tests have deemed it an unfit place to build a home. People have tried building houses there, ignoring the signs and reports that it's an unfit place to build. Needless to say the homes were washed away, leaving nothing but broken remnants scattered along the beach.

If your marriage is like a house, where was the foundation laid? Was it on Washaway Beach—your own ideals of love or feelings of happiness? Or was it built on the stable ground of God's promises and a true understanding of covenant? An oceanfront property on Washaway Beach may seem like it has the best view, but no matter how well you build the house, it won't withstand the storms that will inevitably crash against your foundation.

Having said goodbye to my husband as he went into heart surgery at the age of twenty-two, I am the first to thank God for rescuing and rebuilding our marriage on his solid ground. It wasn't until we came face-to-face with elements that were way out of our control that we recognized exactly where we had built our marriage, and why it wouldn't be a strong enough place to hold us steadfast. In our early years, a lot of our marriage was built on cultural ideals rather than God's Word and his promises. We had built it in what seemed like a beautiful place to live but in reality was Washaway Beach. We desperately needed God to rebuild our foundation on solid ground.

In Matthew 7:24–27 Jesus teaches about the wise builder versus the foolish builder. Let's take a look.

Therefore everyone who hears these words of mine and puts them into practice is like a wise man who built his house on the rock. The rain came down, the streams rose, and the winds blew and beat against that house; yet it did not fall, because it had its foundation on the rock. But everyone who hears these words of mine and does not put them into practice is like a foolish man who built his house on sand. The rain came down, the streams rose, and the winds blew and beat against that house, and it fell with a great crash. (NIV)

So if your marriage is a house, how's your foundation doing? Nothing tests the strength of your marital foundation better than real life. When storms hit (tragedy, sickness, financial ruin), how do you handle them? What if you've lost your job, or your kids are excelling in all things chaotic— Does it feel like your marriage is about to be washed away? There's also the mundane, day-to-day moments of life that seem disenchanting, leaving us unsatisfied and ultimately chipping away at our foundation . . . what then?

No matter how much we try to protect our "home," we can't control the weather. We are fools if we think we can. And when tragedy or hard times come, can our marriage withstand the storm?

What is a strong marital foundation made of? The short answer is Christ. But there is much depth and strength to be had by understanding how *exactly* Christ intends to be the foundation of your marriage. The biblical term for the solid ground under a strong marriage is *covenant*.

The Rock of Covenant

RYAN

Selena makes a potent point: sand is loose and unfixed. Rock is solid and unwavering. Part of building your house on the rock means understanding what covenant means to God and therefore what it *should* mean to you. Basically, a covenant is a set of promises between two people or groups that binds them together. And biblically, a covenant is much more than a contract. It's a bond and promise so strong—so absolute—that only God can give you the means to understand and keep it.

During our first two years as a married couple, we were still in college and I worked as a janitor for the apartment building where we lived. It was a perfect scenario for us. My hours were flexible and we were only about a half-mile walk from campus. This allowed me to provide for my new bride by working full-time while taking a full class load. Selena worked and went to school full-time as well. She'd clock twenty to thirty hours every week at Starbucks and drive thirty minutes each way to the store where she worked. Our schedules were full and so were our hearts.

Quality time together was rare, but we always had at least a little. The quarter waxed on and so did the pressure. Classes grew more intense, work got demanding, and stress mounted. If the first two months of our marriage were filled with joy, the following twenty-two months were filled with varying degrees of fear. The newness of our scrappy newlywed situation faded and the daily grind began taking a toll. My job was a blessing, but I often wondered if it was too good to be true. Though my boss was great, I worried that her patience with me and my class schedule would run out.

I had a total of six floors to keep in tip-top shape at all hours of the day. If ever I faltered in my duties, it was immediately and painfully obvious to management. Trash piled up, dust bunnies appeared, and bathrooms began to stink. It's amazing how quickly chaos could take over—overnight!

Every day I worried I would fail. There was a constant shadow of uncertainty. I went to bed each evening wondering if I missed something or if someone made a huge mess in a far corridor just as I clocked out. Would my boss or an owner see the mess first? Would a resident complain to them in the morning? I lived in constant fear of losing my job. If I got fired everything would be lost, or so I thought. We'd have to move out, quit school, live in a cardboard box—and Selena would probably divorce me! I lived with a never-ending sense of panic that my performance wouldn't be enough.

It feels ridiculous to write those words, especially given all we've been through and where we are now. However, that was my reality and it was tearing me apart.

When I expressed my worry to Selena, she responded perfectly: "Everything will be okay," she said. "God will take care of us. No matter what, I will never stop loving you. We can make it through anything together."

Thank God for Selena! She could have responded so differently. She could have urged me to suck it up and work harder. She could have discounted my stress and told me to just stop obsessing over it. Instead, she affirmed God's sovereignty and reminded me that she wasn't going anywhere. Her words soothed my angst in ways only she could.

What a stark contrast. There I was, working in a job I constantly feared losing while being married to a woman who assured me I could never lose her. That's the difference between a contractual relationship and a covenant promise. It's the difference between performance-based love and love without condition. On one side there is anxiety and on the other there is peace. Fear versus faith.

The greatest freedom to be had in marriage lies, ironically, within the bounds of covenant. There's nothing like it because there's no relationship like marriage.

Your marriage covenant is important to God, not so he can hold it over your heads but so he can express his vast love for you, multiply his joy in you, and amplify his own glory through you.

Covenant in Scripture and the Covenant of Marriage

Building a fierce marriage begins with understanding the higher purpose and context of covenant. There are many Bible passages about marriage, but what if we look at marriage as a unique expression of covenant, which is an overarching theme of the Bible? What is its grander meaning and purpose? What is the big picture of God's covenant relationship with his people, and how should our marriage covenants illustrate God's love?

The entire Bible is an account of God's pursuit of and love for us through the person and work of Jesus Christ. Every book, chapter, and verse adds texture to the story unfolding between God and his people—between Jesus and his Bride.

We serve a God who has always operated through covenant promises. It's his chosen method for relating to his people. Love compelled God to make his covenants, and the same love compels him to keep them. Of the many covenants throughout Scripture, some are conditional: "If you do that, then I will do this." But some of the covenants are unconditional: "I will do this *regardless of what you do*." The gospel is the news that God kept his covenant with his people regardless of what they did—his promise to send a Savior was an unconditional one.

So what kind of covenant is marriage? Simply put, it's conditional. There are two grounds for divorce given in Scripture: sexual immorality (Matt. 5:32; 19:9) and abandonment by an unbeliever (1 Cor. 7:15). In either case, the conditional covenant is considered broken and the believer is permitted to seek divorce.

That being said, God hates divorce and it's never the ideal (Mal. 2:16)—repentance and reconciliation are the ideal (more on that in chapter 9). Aside from the two exceptions provided in Scripture, the marriage covenant is meant to be permanent and unwavering—unconditional in every other way—because through it, we more vividly experience the unconditional love, grace, and forgiveness of God.

Your Marriage Covenant Matters to God—Here's Why

Covenants are a major way that God establishes his sovereignty, displays his everlasting love, and draws his beloved—his people—into deeper relationship with him. From Eden to eternity, every covenant is a pivot point in the story of redemption for God's people in Christ. (See the appendix for a more in-depth discussion of the covenants of Scripture and how they relate to marriage.)

Your marriage covenant is as important to God as his own covenants with his beloved people. He cares about your marriage because he cares about you! The marriage covenant is not an arbitrary framework invented to make your life harder. It is God's design for human flourishing and a tool he uses to mold you and your spouse into images of Christ.

God's covenant with his chosen people—his beloved—is likened repeatedly to a marriage. One of the most vivid examples of this comes from Ezekiel 16: "I made my vow to you and entered into a covenant with you, declares the Lord GOD, and you became mine" (v. 8). This is only a few verses before very strong language rebukes Jerusalem as a "faithless bride"—one who turned from loving adoration and dependence on God to self-sufficiency and idol worship. Like a spurned spouse, God speaks with the intense love, emotion, and commitment of one who loves covenantally:

> For thus says the Lord GOD: I will deal with you as you have done, you who have despised the oath in breaking the covenant, yet I will remember my covenant with you in the days of your youth, and I will establish for you an everlasting covenant. . . . And you shall know that I am the LORD, that you may remember and be confounded, and never open your mouth again because of your shame, when I atone for you for all that you have done, declares the Lord GOD. (vv. 59–60, 62–63)

Even in God's heartache (if I can call it that), he foreshadowed the atoning grace to be given to the church through Jesus, the ultimate Bridegroom, in order to present to himself a blameless Bride—his chosen people.

Just as promised, God sent his Son Jesus to atone for sin and reconcile us to him. After Jesus ascended into heaven, the disciples began preparing his Bride—the church—for the ultimate wedding.

It was while establishing the early church that the apostle Paul wrote some of the most potent instructions for marriage found in the New Testament. He instructed believers to conduct themselves within marriage and family according to Christ's love for his church. Paul, being very well educated, certainly understood the overwhelming parallel as he wrote to believers in Ephesus. He directly compared the love between a husband and wife to that between Christ and his Bride, the church. Read the passage below carefully in light of God's covenantal character:

> Wives, submit to your own husbands, as to the Lord. For the husband is the head of the wife even as Christ is the head of the church, his body, and is himself its Savior. Now as the church submits to Christ, so also wives should submit in everything to their husbands.
>
> Husbands, love your wives, as Christ loved the church and gave himself up for her, that he might sanctify her, having cleansed her by the washing of water with the word, so that he might present the church to himself in splendor, without spot or wrinkle or any such thing, that she might be holy and without blemish. In the same way husbands should love their wives as their own bodies. He who loves his wife loves himself. For no one ever hated his own flesh, but nourishes and cherishes it, just as Christ does the church, because we are members of his body. "Therefore a man shall leave his father and mother and hold fast to his wife, and the two shall become one flesh." This mystery is profound, and I am saying that it refers to Christ and the church. However, let each one of you love his wife as himself, and let the wife see that she respects her husband. (Eph. 5:22–33)

Husbands are called to love as Christ loved the church, and wives are called to trust and submit as the church submits to Christ. Without context Paul's words are enough to make women cringe and men hide under a rock. Within the context of covenant and God's character in Christ, Paul's words paint a beautiful, vivid picture of mutual, covenantal love.

Indeed, the full depth of the above passage and those similar to it are the subject of this book, but for now I want us to grasp the bigger picture: God designed marriage as a covenant because it's the only framework strong enough to sustain it, and when we honor it, we flourish. But it won't always be easy.

It's during the hardest times in marriage when we most vividly experience the covenantal nature and relentless pursuit of God. He never gave up on his people despite their infidelity, and he will never give up on you. No matter how far you wander, the Good Shepherd will always find you and carry you home. No matter how you spend his grace, it will never run out. Marriage requires a similar resolve and fierce tenacity to not give up on each other when things get difficult.

Your covenant binds you together so you have nowhere to go except to Christ for help and back to each other for reconciliation. It will keep you near one another when you have nothing else to give or take but mercy and grace. Finally, it opens your eyes and softens your heart to the immeasurable need you have for unending grace, your inability to earn it, and the steep price by which it is given.

Much like the gospel produces joy, the experience of grace within marriage begets more love, creates more joy, and inspires truer intimacy. Covenant love puts you in the thick of God's grace—you experience it in full color and HD detail.

The Three Purposes of the Marriage Covenant

God calls your marriage a covenant on purpose, *for his purposes*. But what purposes does God have in mind? We get a glimpse by looking back to the beginning. Deep in Eden, just after speaking everything into existence, God made humankind his crowning creation:

> Then God said, "Let us make man in our image, after our likeness. And let them have dominion over the fish of the sea and over the birds of the heavens and over the livestock and over all the earth and over every creeping thing that creeps on the earth."
>
> > So God created man in his own image,
> > in the image of God he created him;
> > male and female he created them.
>
> And God blessed them. And God said to them, "Be fruitful and multiply and fill the earth and subdue it." (Gen. 1:26–28)

Picture what this must have looked like! The garden teemed with diverse life. Beasts of every kind ran freely through the soft and fragrant air, which was undoubtedly filled with aromas and pollens of an unimaginable mix of trees and flowers. Every aspect of God's creation was perfectly designed and flawlessly attested to his glory. Then, from the same dust and dirt he used to make every living thing, God created humankind. Except this creation was different—it was special.

God gave man and woman three unique mandates immediately after creating them: be fruitful, multiply, and subdue the earth (Gen. 1:28). If we read the parallel account in Genesis 2, this happens during the same moment when God united the two as "one flesh" and said the man would "hold fast to his wife" (v. 24). It is within the context of their divine union that God expected them to carry out his first commands. He prepared them for his work by creating them, *then* joining them together.

This isn't to say that unmarried people cannot bring glory to God; they can and do. But it was after their unification and to them *as a pair* that God gave Adam and Eve their first directives. Those three instructions begin to reveal God's larger purposes for every marriage.

Purpose 1: Your Holiness—"Be Fruitful"

The "be fruitful" command is profound in the context of creation. Remember that it was given before the fall, part of the intended state of things. Everything flawlessly reflected God's glory, and humanity was in perfect relationship with him. Plants bore fruit by design, and in doing so, replicated themselves and existed exactly as God intended. In a way, plants were also commanded to "bear fruit" when God spoke them into existence and designed their cells to reproduce. Bearing fruit is a sign of an organism's health, its purpose.

Fruitfulness is an idea often used in the Bible to describe the health of the Christian life. Spiritual fruit is a consistent indicator of faith in Christ and the indwelling of the Holy Spirit. Horticulture is a biblical theme used to illustrate the purpose of human existence and warn against pitfalls.

Jesus said, "Abide in me, and I in you. As the branch cannot bear fruit by itself, unless it abides in the vine, neither can you, unless you abide in me" (John 15:4), and "Either make the tree good and its fruit good, or make the tree bad and its fruit bad; for the tree is known by its fruit" (Matt. 12:33). John the Baptist warned listeners, "Even now the axe is laid to the root of the trees. Every tree therefore that does not bear good fruit is cut down and thrown into the fire" (Luke 3:9). He also said Jesus would soon arrive to "clear his threshing floor and to gather the wheat into his barn, but the chaff he will burn with unquenchable fire" (v. 17). He was speaking to Pharisees who had come to rest on their heritage and good works as their source of justification before God.

God is our gardener, and he wants his people to bear good fruit. Under Mosaic law this expectation was crushing and unreachable. But Jesus changed everything! He fulfilled the old law, and now we live justified in him. It is from that *life in Christ's justification* that Paul urges believers to bear "fruit of the Spirit": love, joy, peace, patience, kindness, goodness, faithfulness, gentleness, and self-control (Gal. 5:22–23).

So we must not pass too quickly over those two words in Genesis, "be fruitful." It was *a command given to a unified man and woman*—a husband and his wife. But how is marriage integral in making us holy and helping us bear godly fruit?

God uses marriage to produce fruit in you and make you more like Christ. Like most, Selena and I had no idea how vital our vows were when we said them. The security and certainty of our covenant to each other has created the space for our sanctification. Neither of us has to be perfect to still be loved by the other. We know that we can make mistakes and we always have the room to work through them. We can repent to each other, confess our sin and doubt, and know that the other person won't quit. Your marriage covenant is meant to be a safe venue for real, unfiltered life and a place of relentless, unbridled commitment.

It is within the safety of your marriage covenant where the fires of sanctification can be cranked up. It is a beautiful thing. When I mess up and Selena asks me about it, I don't have to lie. I don't have to struggle alone. I am free to confess and be honest, standing secure in her promise to me and her commitment to keeping it. I often tell my wife there is nothing she can do to get rid of me. Depending on her mood and my level of obnoxiousness that day, she may or may not be happy to hear it!

Purpose 2: Your Household—"Multiply"

Your marriage covenant is also your context for multiplication. And I'm not just talking about making babies. Sure, that's a huge part of it (which we'll discuss), but multiplication in the Christian life means so much more.

Marriage is the foundation for generational flourishing. It encapsulates both the conception of children and raising them into self-sufficient, God-honoring adults. The holy union of one man and one woman, just as Adam and Eve were united, reveals to generations the spectrum of God's nature. The characteristics of God revealed in the wife are complementary to those made visible in the husband. The husband is called to headship of his household, leading lovingly and with grace. Through the gospel, wives are empowered to honor and respect their godly husbands, not as a mark of weakness but as one of the utmost strength.

Our children are meant to witness godly marriage and in that way encounter the character of God in a simple and profound manner. It is through seeing the love between one's parents that a child becomes acquainted with the love of Christ years before hearing the gospel.

Your marriage is also a stable platform for discipleship—inside and outside the home. When God told Adam and Eve to "multiply" in the garden, he was saying, "Go, continue this work I've completed." He wanted to see his perfect image of creation perpetuated through them. I believe we're oversimplifying if we assume this only applied to their natural bodies. God created man from the dust, stitching together the physical pieces in intricate detail. Next, he "breathed into his nostrils the breath of life, and the man became a living creature" (Gen. 2:7). Just as God created Adam's body, he made his soul. Marriage is meant to be our exclusive context for physical multiplication but it is a major avenue for spiritual multiplication as well.

Selena and I often remind ourselves that our first disciples are our kids. If we're not telling them about Jesus, something is terribly wrong! Next, we are called to "multiply" by discipling others intentionally—both individuals and couples. Just as many have poured into us over the years, we are called to "perpetuate God's design"—his desire to be in perfect relationship, now possible once again through Christ—by discipling others.

The call to make disciples is not exclusive to married couples, but it seems clear that marriage is one way God equips the called. It is this process of spiritual multiplication that brings us to the final purpose of marriage: God's handiwork.

Purpose 3: God's Handiwork—"Subdue the Earth"

We are called to be fruitful, multiply, and, finally, subdue the earth. God's final charge in Eden is a powerful one. Without being given God's specific blessing—his *permission*—to have dominion over the earth, we would have no right to work or do anything with or within creation. It is the one command out of the three that doesn't apply to any of God's other creatures; it only applies to humanity. But what exactly are we given permission to do? And what does marriage have to do with it?

This command, like the others, was given as Adam and Eve were unified in marriage, and they were meant to carry it out as a team. Their responsibility to care for and enjoy the produce of the earth was God's continuation of the creative act—his perpetual handiwork—and he allowed Adam and Eve to participate.

Though we are marred by sin, this is still our reality after the fall. God is still at work and he calls us to participate. God is actively rescuing and redeeming his children. Throughout Scripture God uses imperfect people to accomplish his purposes. The same is true for us today. God wants to use us for his glory. That call, though not exclusive to married couples, is uniquely applicable to them.

A few years back, Selena and I realized that our marriage could be our ministry. As we've grown more unified, our ministry has strengthened. In the years before this shift, we'd do our own things and serve in different ways. God was gracious and allowed us to be fruitful as individuals, but we've discovered a power in unity when we minister together that amplifies our effectiveness. We subdue the earth together as we invite couples to our home, raise our babies from a unified front, and respond to convictions God gives each of us for how else we should minister.

Our friends Joel and Rachael define the word *radical*. They're parents, world travelers, ministers of the gospel, and advocates for the forgotten. Joel runs a nonprofit called Nations Foundation, which tells stories of gospel-centered reformers around the world. They subdue the earth by going to the far reaches of the world (sometimes together, sometimes separately), getting their hands dirty, learning cultural complexities, and telling the stories of those who are doing

Christ's work in the darkest places. There is no way they could do what they do without total unity in their marriage—the kind that can only be explained by the call of Christ on their lives. God has used them in unique and mighty ways, and their marriage covenant has only bolstered their work for the gospel.

As a married couple, you have a unique opportunity to subdue the earth and continue God's handiwork. Just as God uses your marriage to produce fruit in you ("be fruitful") and through you ("multiply"), he is calling you to continue his work by helping others produce good fruit ("subdue the earth").

Covenant of Love

By now we hope you better understand the deep meaning of covenant and how God's purposes are accomplished through marriage. Knowing this much will give you context and reason to fight fiercely through every struggle you'll encounter as a couple.

We must grasp that marriage is a covenant of extreme importance and a concept birthed in the mind of God. Next to trusting Jesus, whom you marry and how you navigate your marriage are the most important decisions you will ever make. Your marriage covenant is deeply personal and spiritually vital. It is a magnificent part of God's plan in the world around you and inside of you. The purpose of your marriage is both lofty and familiar, eternal and daily, earthly and heavenly.

If all of this sounds grandiose, that's because it is! Marriage is incredibly important. It's serious business and everything is at stake. That is not to say God's grace doesn't abound—because it does, it *always* does. It is to say that we must not forget the weight of covenant, the importance of marriage, and its purposes in accomplishing God's work.

Perhaps you're still surprised that we've said so much about one biblical theme—covenant—and so little about another—love. That's because the word *love* is tossed around so thoughtlessly with regard to marriage. Only now, with a clear idea of covenant, can we move on to talk about covenant love. That kind of love has a quality you don't hear about in greeting cards—a quality we can only call *gritty*.

FOR REFLECTION

- Do you believe God's design for covenantal marriage is the best route for human flourishing? Why or why not?
- We mentioned three purposes of covenant in marriage. How do you currently see these at work in your marriage?
- Is there a particular covenant purpose you struggle with? Why?

4

Gritty Love

It's Everything You Think and More

> To be loved but not known is comforting but superficial. To be known and not loved is our greatest fear. But to be fully known and truly loved is, well, a lot like being loved by God.
>
> Timothy Keller

I first noticed Selena while visiting her school in eighth grade. It was a small Christian school in a suburban farm town just south of Seattle. My mom was interviewing for an open vice principal job, so I spent the day comingling with unfamiliar students. To be honest, I mostly stayed silent. I was a very shy kid.

My church friend, Phil, was a student there, and we arranged for him to show me around, except he wouldn't be there until 10:00 a.m. The first class was underway when my mom and I arrived, so the office staff figured it best for me to sit in on gym class. At least then I could sneak in quietly and avoid interrupting the teacher. Comforted with stealth and anonymity, I sat in the corner of the gym on a rolled up wrestling mat.

The students were playing a game that looked like a combination of basketball, football, and ultimate Frisbee. I shuffled through my backpack and pulled out a book to read for one of my own classes. I needed the time to catch up on some homework and welcomed the temporary isolation.

Then I looked up and my life changed forever. There she was. *Selena*.

I can still remember that moment so vividly. I can even feel how it felt. Time itself seemed to slow down. Her long brown hair had been pulled into a ponytail. She carried herself with confidence and sureness that I found captivating. My heart dropped clear through the soles of my shoes, and I spent the rest of the class trying to casually catch glimpses of her without creeping her out.

Gym class ended and Phil finally showed up. He told me her name and we proceeded toward the next class for the day.

Again, there she was! Except this time she was even more beautiful than I realized. My insides were in knots. I felt weirdly despondent, consumed with that lovesickness teenage boys get when a girl is utterly compelling but hopelessly out of reach. This was especially true for me. There was Selena, practically perfect in every way (or so I thought), and then there was me: awkward, quiet, a little weird-looking, and smack-dab in the middle of puberty.

I had liked girls before but this was somehow different—very different. I remember thinking, *Is this . . . love?* It certainly felt like it.

I never found the courage to speak to Selena that day, but she proved unforgettable. When the school day was over, I left but she remained in my thoughts. Little did I realize that I had just seen for the first time the woman I'd spend my life pursuing.

Was it love at first sight? You *could* call it that. Maybe I had just experienced a fresh flood of teenage hormones. Either way, I was sold.

Fast-forward six months: my mom got the job, and I started ninth grade at Selena's school. My feelings only intensified. Not only was she stunningly beautiful but she was also an accomplished student. She served on student council, took advanced placement classes, and carried herself with a friendly confidence unlike anyone I'd ever met. She wasn't shy like me; she knew how to speak in front of people. She was a leader and a good one.

I was an awkward introvert who preferred listening to Pearl Jam and playing my guitar alone in my bedroom over social interaction. I wouldn't have been caught dead speaking in front of class. I was the kind of kid no one noticed when I walked into a room. If someone did notice me and happen to ask my name, they would immediately forget it.

It wasn't until a full year after that fateful moment in the gymnasium that I spoke to Selena for the first time. Our initial exchange was thrilling (at least for me). I could tell she was just being friendly to the new kid in school, but I was doing reconnaissance. I was studying her. I was learning all about her and starting what would eventually become a lifetime of pursuit.

My heart ached to be important to Selena. I wanted to be known. More importantly, I wanted to know her deeply. I could have called it love at the time, but I now realize how little I understood what the word *love* meant or what it would cost.

Now, what seems like a lifetime later, we're married and have babies. I still feel like I'm barely starting to grasp what it means to love her the way I should, which ideally is out of the covenant we made with each other on our wedding day. When you commit to covenant love, you don't just observe love from a distance; you walk in it. Covenant love is not as easy as I anticipated.

As it turns out, committing to love another human being forever is hard and messy. But by God's design and grace, marriage provides the perfect venue for our love to deepen. If we make light of the marital covenant, we make light of love itself. Covenant love is weighty; it has substance. Without knowing it, we can too quickly choose convenient love over covenant love. Covenant love takes grit. It is not easy, cheap, or ready to retreat at any sign of trouble. Covenant love is deep, unwavering, unconditional, and decided. It's how God loves us, and it provides us with the answers to hard questions like "Did I 'fall in love' with Selena that morning in the gymnasium?" I don't think so. I prefer to call it the moment our love began. Questions rooted in fear like "Will I fall out of love with her at some point?" are answered by covenant love. First John 4:18 reminds us that "there is no fear in love, but perfect love casts out fear. For fear has to do with punishment, and whoever fears has not been perfected in love."

Covenant love costs more than we can ever realize before the moment payment is due. It costs pride, time, effort, selfishness, and so much more. But that's the beauty of covenant love: it's a choice you can make even when you feel like doing the opposite, and you're never without a clear definition of what it means to love, nor is it up to you to muster the power to walk in it. God gives us a Helper (the Holy Spirit) and his Word to help guide us in covenant love.

Rest in your covenant with each other; relax and understand that it's in place to give your love a venue in which to mature into something more and more representative of Christ's love for his Bride—the church.

If Christ is the bedrock of a thriving marriage (and he is), understanding *covenant love* is the foundation. Thus far we've discussed the covenant part of that statement: the weight of it and its importance to God. However, much of how you live within your marital covenant depends not only on understanding what covenant is but also knowing what *love* is. Love's definition may seem obvious, but as we'll see, it's not. Because of that, we must be clear—even the slightest misunderstanding of what love is can devastate the strongest marriage.

Plain as Day, Clear as Mud

Love saturates virtually every facet of modern culture. It's everywhere—in music, literature, media, even politics. Given the stark emphasis society places on love, it's shocking how uncertain the definition still is. I'm not talking about the dictionary definition of love (*noun: an intense feeling of deep affection*) but rather a definition that *actually* mirrors reality—one that accurately and sufficiently describes the *one thing* humanity has longed to experience more desperately and consistently than any other concept or idea.

Simply put, what do we mean when we say "I love you"?

SoulPancake is a "positive and inspiring media and entertainment company" that creates content for YouTube and cable networks. They recently produced a video with the sole aim of defining love. They interviewed dozens of individuals ranging in age from five to one hundred and five and asked them one simple question: What is love? As people answered, they struggled to articulate verbally what was so clearly reflected in their eyes. You can almost see the moments their mental gears grind to a halt when trying to find the words.

Their ad-hoc responses are not only fascinating but I believe they're a representative snapshot of our present culture's perspective on love:

> "Love means never having to say you're sorry—but I don't believe that at all because I feel like you say you're sorry a lot." (thirty-four-year-old woman)

> "Someone who loves you, loves you because—you're you." (eleven-year-old girl)

> "Love means accepting people the way they are." (sixty-four-year-old man)

> "It has to be a two-way street. It can't just be . . . you know . . . I'm accepting you. You gotta accept me too." (fifty-year-old woman)

> "Love to me is something you do on a day-to-day basis. You can hold affection and you can hold nostalgia, but I think love is active." (thirty-two-year-old woman)

> "I always say I'd rather love someone than *be* in love with someone. Because being *in love* with someone implies that you can fall out of it." (nineteen-year-old man)[1]

As you can see, responses were widely varied. Each reply echoed some aspect of truth, but as I watched I could tell that none of them completely satisfied the person answering.

They struggled to put words to what they knew in their guts. This is not a new phenomenon. Psychologists, philosophers, and scientists have been wrestling with the concept of love for all of human history.

Loveology

Robert Sternberg of Yale University provides a compelling vision of love in his theory called "The Triangular Theory of Love."[2] In his paper he aims to answer the question "What does it mean to love someone?" Sternberg's love model identifies three key components that help us understand it: intimacy, passion, and commitment. In the study, intimacy represents emotional closeness and caring, passion includes emotional or physical excitement (arousal), and commitment refers to a decision to *try* to maintain love over a period of time.

Sternberg describes eight types of love that occur when you mix and match varying degrees of intimacy, passion, and commitment in a relationship. The types range from "non-love" relationships that have none of the aspects to "romantic love" that has passion and intimacy but no commitment. Of all the types of love Sternberg proposed, the one that most closely resembles what we're called to in a biblical marriage is the only type that includes all three components. He called it *consummate*, or complete, love. Those in a consummate love relationship express intimacy, passion, *and* commitment to one another with consistency and equality. This, in his view, is the most complete type of love possible in a relationship. Shocking discovery, I know, but at the very least he puts words to what most people desire intuitively and struggle to articulate.

Sternberg is just one of countless thinkers throughout history who have tried to define, once and for all, the human phenomenon called *love*. Some of them have reduced love to a series of neurons firing in the brain and others discuss it in terms of anthropology or sociology—it's the result of evolutionary processes that helped humanity survive and multiply. Just to name a few.

Our academic understanding of love is further along than ever before, yet society is still confused. That's because love isn't like other hard sciences where A plus B always equals C; it's much more complicated than that.

The Art and Science of Love

Most often, we define love subjectively, just like the people did in the SoulPancake video. Much of how they defined love had to do with their own observations or expectations of it—and that's fine! In many ways love *is* subjective. It's a mixture of feelings, thoughts, desires, actions, and responses to another human being. When expressing love in marriage you experience many of its subjective characteristics. You might feel elated when your spouse walks through the door. Your heart drops when he or she catches you off guard with an honest kiss. You think of each other often, plan surprise date nights, and show affection in ways that are unique to your relationship. Those expressions of love are good and beautiful! There's a reason that the best songs and poems are often about love—in many ways, love is art.

What keeps us from following every whim and feeling that makes our heart drop or our knees weak? The answer is simple: life wouldn't go well if we did. Though wonderful, feelings aren't predictable, and building a lasting marriage requires something solid. We need something tangible and absolute—something objective.

How we *feel* doesn't always align with what we know about love. When our feelings don't align with what we know, we must choose to love despite how we feel—we must act on what we *know* love is. Love gets objective really fast within the marriage covenant. It's where our love's true grittiness shines through.

Marriage is unique; there is no other human relationship that will more exhaustively test our understanding of what it means to love another person. If you're like us, you've fought to love each other in your marriage but have often fallen short. Where is the disconnect? If we know what love is and we naturally desire it, why do we miss the mark? Why do we still express frustration in ways that are hurtful? Why do we neglect to give one another what we know we both need? Why do our actions of love fall short of our understanding of it? If "love never fails," why does it . . . fail?

The deepest disagreements you will experience as a married couple always have to do with your objective view of love and the expectations that come along with it. That view determines how you will act when wronged, how you will ask for forgiveness when you sin against each other, how you serve one another selflessly (or don't), and how generous you are with each other.

This materialized early on in our marriage whenever we'd argue about quality time. Selena needs quality time to feel loved—she thrives on it. I don't need it as much, and I'd often work late into the evening thinking that I *was* actively loving her—by providing. Eventually she'd bring it up and I'd get defensive. I'd insist, "I'm working longer hours to provide for you!" Though she was grateful, she had to find a way to remind me that none of it mattered if we didn't have time together. She felt utterly unloved if I was absent. I felt unloved if my work went unappreciated. We both wanted to give and receive love, but it was like we were using completely different currencies. How we've grown since those early days has only come with plenty of trial and lots of error—and we're still far from perfection.

That's precisely why we need to carefully define love, and to do that we must look outside of ourselves. We need an external standard. We must ask Someone who holds all authority in defining love itself.

The Measuring Standard

Ancient Corinth was the booming capital city of Achaia, a Roman province that made up most of modern-day Greece. Its dusty, bustling streets were filled with sounds of bartering shop owners and ox-drawn carts. Because of its strategic economic location, Corinth was a center for trade both by sea and by land. As a result, the city was ruled by extravagant wealth and raw worldliness. The pagan culture of ancient Greece was alive and prolific. A few miles from the city, Acrocorinth Mountain stood nineteen hundred feet tall. On its summit was the temple of Aphrodite, the goddess of love, and at its base was the temple of Palaemon, "the guardian of ships."[3] Corinth was as worldly as it was booming, and it was here that God saw fit to reach people through Paul's planting of a local church.

Paul first visited Corinth after his stay in Athens (Acts 17) and spent an unusually long period of eighteen months evangelizing and ministering to new believers there. He then left the new church in the hands of able elders and continued on his missionary journey to Syria and Ephesus. After some time away Paul received a troubling report from the Corinthian church. He wrote 1 Corinthians—including his famous love chapter—in response. What exactly was Paul responding to?

In the brief time since Paul's departure, the Corinthian church began to stray from the gospel. Culture and sin shifted their doctrine, degraded their morality, and divided their congregation. Believers condoned blatant sexual immorality within the church, filed lawsuits against one another in pagan courts, and overindulged themselves at the Lord's Supper (among other things). Paul boldly and systematically addressed these issues throughout 1 Corinthians, and he did so without holding back—and with a voice of challenging compassion.

In chapter 12 Paul talked about spiritual gifts held by individuals in the church. The Corinthians had come to laud certain spiritual gifts over others, which alienated some believers and exalted others. Paul corrected this wrong behavior by affirming the vitality of every gift—every person—within the body of Christ (vv. 6, 18, 20). Paul closed the chapter by reminding them that they could not all bear the same gifts, nor should they! Instead, they should "earnestly desire the higher gifts" (v. 31). His last statement before moving on to the "love chapter" was this: "And I will show you a still more excellent way," namely, love.

Then Paul wrote chapter 13, the unforgettable "love chapter" we hear so often at weddings. He was compelled to clearly describe love because they were missing the mark completely. The Corinthian church was so steeped in culture that they had forgotten what it meant to love one another in light of the gospel. Their definition of love had shifted to an enabling tolerance of sin, overindulgence, and prideful arrogance toward one another. They needed to hit the reset button and relearn "the more excellent way." They needed to be reminded of the definition of love. Does the culture in Corinth sound familiar? Paul wrote:

> Love is patient, love is kind. It does not envy, it does not boast, it is not proud. It does not dishonor others, it is not self-seeking, it is not easily angered, it keeps no record of wrongs. Love does not delight in evil but rejoices with the truth. It always protects, always trusts, always hopes, always perseveres.
> Love never fails. (1 Cor. 13:4–8 NIV)

We, too, need reminders. We so easily forget what it truly means to love if we place too much weight on our culture's definition. When affection and feelings wane, does it mean we are falling out of love? If we're struggling in our sex life, is the passion gone and love lost forever? If I'm deeply wronged, am I justified to cut the ties and run? If my spouse fails too often or is less than I'd hoped, can I just leave?

The imperfect moments in your marriage are your most potent opportunities to love fully. That kind of bare, unrelenting love is the "more excellent way" Paul is talking about.

Paul's words would have been jarring to the Corinthian church. He knew the Corinthians intimately, having spent considerable time discipling, teaching, and instructing the early gatherers. He'd introduced them to the good news of the gospel, witnessed their facial expressions as it sank in, and rejoiced with them as they put their trust in Jesus for the first time. His reminder in 1 Corinthians 13 would have felt like a harsh reprimand from a father who knew they knew better and was disappointed in their rejection of wisdom.

Paul's list of love's attributes is daunting, and if we take it seriously we may doubt our ability to ever meet love's demands. If that's you, take a deep breath and relax. You don't have to be perfect. God is faithfully at work on your heart, teaching you how to love more completely—how to be patient, kind, humble, considerate, selfless, and so much more. We will never love our spouses perfectly on this side of eternity, but God also never stops showing us how.

Finding the Power to Love

I once heard a story of a little boy who was struggling to lift a heavy rock. His father came along just then. Noting the boy's failure, he asked, "Are you using all your strength?"

"Yes, I am," the little boy said impatiently.

"No, you are not," the father answered. "I am right here just waiting, and you haven't asked me to help you."

As much as we may want to, we can't muster the will to love, at least not for long. I can't count the number of times I've promised Selena—and myself—that I'd change my actions and be a "better man," only to fall short after a few days (if I even make it that long). I've held back words during frustrating moments only to have those same words sprout bitterness and resentment in my heart as I stuff them away. Inevitably, they erupt in unhealthy explosions of anger and hurtful communication. I can resolve to *be* better all I want, but change will never stick until the gospel transforms my heart.

After my surgery, I was—to put it bluntly—a huge jerk to Selena. I don't know what it was, but something changed my personality for a time. I was impatient, bitter, quick to anger, and horrible at articulating how I felt. My behavior didn't change until God showed me the power of my words in Selena's heart and convicted me to love her well by speaking lovingly—intentionally. I felt the Holy Spirit lead me in when to be silent and when to speak. He showed me how to be tender by opening my eyes to his tenderness toward me. He taught me patience by revealing how patient he is with me. He changed me from the inside out.

Every lasting change in our hearts is the result of God's work, not our own.

The power to truly and selflessly love each other in marriage only comes from experiencing God's grace in Christ, and by the power of the Holy Spirit. It is by understanding our dire need for a Savior and hearing the good news of Christ's saving grace that true love wells up within us and spills out into every facet of life. This pattern is evident throughout Scripture, particularly (again) in the early church.

As the news about Jesus spread throughout ancient Asia, churches sprang up. Just as Paul wrote to the Corinthians, the apostle John wrote a series of letters to congregants in Asia to encourage them in the faith. In his first letter we read a potent call to love:

> Beloved, let us love one another, for love is from God, and whoever loves has been born of God and knows God. Anyone who does not love does not know God, because God is love. (1 John 4:7–8)

Before proceeding we must make two vital distinctions about this passage. First, the love John mentions is not prescriptive, it's descriptive. He's not *prescribing* a way to be "born of God." Rather, John is *describing* what a person "born of God" looks like. He says, "By this we know . . ." (v. 13). It's as if he's looking at a picture of love and simply telling us what he sees. Love toward another is a natural result of being born of God. Knowing God is the cause, love is the effect. This subtle difference dramatically changes how we love each other and root out problems when we fall short.

The second important distinction is that Scripture says "God is love" not "love is God" (v. 8). This is especially relevant for modern culture, as we tend to create an idol out of love itself, giving our idea of love full authority to override other directives from God. The love of God is inseparable from the rest of his character. God is holy, just, *loving*, merciful, and so many other things; he is all of them, all at once. His character is unchanging and unwavering.

We know we've made an idol of love when we sacrifice the other characteristics of God on its altar. For example, an unmarried couple might choose to live together and sleep together because they "love" each other. When challenged on their lifestyle by a pastor or counselor because they are living in sin, they might respond, "We love each other, and God knows we're committed." They have let their definition of love override God's commands regarding sex and covenant marriage. Love becomes our god when it is used to justify breaking the commands of God. Love is not a god. *God is love*, but he is also holy and just.

Love Personified

God's ultimate love was proven to us through Christ's life, death, and resurrection. Christ is the literal personification of God's love, and it is only through trusting him that we experience and are able to give true, lasting, 1 Corinthians 13 love to our spouse.

Jesus's love is gritty and pure. He met the needs of the people around him through healing, miraculously providing food, and ultimately giving his life so that we might be saved. He humbly left a perfect heaven to come down to redeem and save a broken world. He wasn't forced to carry the cross; he did so willingly.

God knows the cost of love more than we will ever understand. To find the power to love we must make Christ the ultimate target of our love and understand how he is the perfect lover of our souls. He is the ultimate example of patience and waits lovingly at your heart's door for an invitation in. When invited, he will come in and eat with you, and you with him (Rev. 3:20). Christ shows us kindness, just as he did with the Samaritan woman at the well (John 4:7). He *sees* us for who we really are even when we fail to recognize his lordship. He knows our history, our sin, and our failures, yet he generously offers himself to us.

Jesus is never arrogant or rude. He dined with social outcasts and sinners because he loved them; in the same way, he would dine with you and me. He is a Good Shepherd, tending to your wounds, cleaning clots of mud and excrement from your wool, and carrying you home. He sees every inch of you, in all your sheepy filthiness, lost and lame, and still he desires you and chooses to rescue you—only to rejoice when you're returned home!

Jesus was selfless, his will totally aligned with the Father's. Though fully man, he never insisted on his own way. He rejoiced in doing the will of the Father, even as he walked the path to the cross.

Jesus does not grow irritable or resentful with you when you fail to grasp or apply his teaching. He patiently instructs in ways you can understand, often through parables and stories.

Jesus never fails and never ends. He was there at the dawn of time (John 1:1) and he will remain for all eternity; his presence and power know no bounds. The same is true for his love.

Can you see it? Can you *feel* it? Jesus is our only reliable definition and source of real love. We must cling to him first, carefully discarding worldly definitions that don't align with who he is or how he loves. Christ alone is perfect love personified: God sent his only Son, whom he loved beyond comprehension, not just to die but to die a painful death and suffer separation. The weight of God's love multiplies as we remember that Jesus is God in the flesh.

The only explanation for the cross is God's covenant love. It is deeper and wider than we will ever understand. It goes beyond all convenience, comfort, and human convention. The love you express in your marriage is meant to be a reflection of God's covenant love for his people. Your marriage will flourish when Christ becomes your absolute standard and context for loving each other. Anything else is rooted in convenience rather than covenant. God is calling you to something richer, deeper, and vastly more fulfilling than convenient love; God is calling you to covenant love.

The Love in-between Moments

SELENA

So how do Ryan and I experience covenant love in our marriage? How does it function in our day to day? One way that's helped me recognize it is simply by seeing my husband through the 1 Corinthians 13 lens. In other words, where has he been patient and kind with me when, in reality, he had all the right to be frustrated and angry? Where has he been selfless, courteous, and hopeful toward me? When I look at why he chooses to love me when I prove over and over to be difficult to love, my heart is grateful. I know Ryan's love is not based on me; it's anchored in Christ's love and the covenant we made to each other on our wedding day.

Over the years of our marriage, it's been the moments between the big romantic landmarks that really count. Like the one where I popped a car tire by hitting a curb (Ryan says I always drive too close to them) and everything inside me didn't want to tell him. But I did, and instead of starting a big blowup fight, he surprised me with patience and kindness. Those are the moments I point to and say, "There! There is where I experienced Ryan's love!" Or when he makes us all breakfast even though I know he has a ton of work to get done—another in-between, mundane moment of loving me, loving our family. I experience Ryan's love through his patience with me in my angry moments. His selfless pursuit of me, despite feeling hurt by me, helps me experience his love.

One area I've experienced this in is our sex life. Having two kiddos requires us to plan and strategize more about when we can be intimate. All too often our every-two-to-three-day goal of having sex will go unnoticed by me. Neither of us initiates because I'm typically tired, and he hears me expressing my tiredness, which leads to his feeling hurt and unloved because physical touch is his primary love language. Ryan could easily make me feel guilty for not meeting his needs or making him feel loved, but he doesn't. Instead he lovingly communicates his feelings and needs to me, his wife, which diffuses the whole situation. He couldn't actively or selflessly love or pursue me like this without having first experienced 1 Corinthians 13 love from Jesus.

It's important to note that nowhere in the love chapter does the passage label love as a feeling. Feelings come and go, emotions fade, but God's love for us is never failing and unconditional. He relentlessly pursues our souls.

Let's trust God to define love. By sending his Son Jesus to die in our place, he gave what we could not because he loves us. He continues to provide all that we need: acceptance, love, security, and hope. When we believe, really believe, this to be true about God's nature, we can't help but serve and appreciate our spouse every day, no matter the circumstance. Let's continue on this journey of understanding God's love and allow it to fill our souls so that *out* of his love for us we can better love our spouse.

Thirsty Marriage

A marriage rooted in Christ is not without hardship, but the joy and fulfillment experienced because of the hardship bears witness to our souls that without Jesus, our marriage will get tired and heavy. There's a lot of noise in our world today about how to alleviate burdens and pain through positive thinking and actions. These messages put all the pressure on what we should *do* rather than simply *receiving* from God, our Living Water. In other words, we are drawing from our own strength (which will inevitably fall short) instead of recognizing our desperate need for a Savior and, in turn, walking out the reality of the gospel with our divine Helper day to day.

In John 4, Jesus meets a Samaritan woman at a well and asks her for a drink. He takes the opportunity to help her recognize her "thirst," her need for a Savior and Helper. He gives, she receives, and she lives out of what she received.

> When a Samaritan woman came to draw water, Jesus said to her, "Will you give me a drink?" (His disciples had gone into the town to buy food.)
>
> The Samaritan woman said to him, "You are a Jew and I am a Samaritan woman. How can you ask me for a drink?" (For Jews do not associate with Samaritans.)
>
> Jesus answered her, "If you knew the gift of God and who it is that asks you for a drink, you would have asked him and he would have given you living water."
>
> "Sir," the woman said, "you have nothing to draw with and the well is deep. Where can you get this living water? Are you greater than our father Jacob, who gave us the well and drank from it himself, as did also his sons and his livestock?"
>
> Jesus answered, "Everyone who drinks this water will be thirsty again, but whoever drinks the water I give them will never thirst. Indeed, the water I give them will become in them a spring of water welling up to eternal life." (John 4:7–14 NIV)

When we get to know Jesus and understand who he is and the message he brings, like the Samaritan woman, we begin to understand how thirsty our marriage is. We're thirsty for a Savior who will forgive our selfish actions, and we're thirsty for the Holy Spirit who will empower us to love. That's what living water is: the Savior and the Spirit. We need only to receive and then live and love out of the work of the Holy Spirit.

Of course, even if we're committed to covenant love, temptations will still try to draw us off track. Our marriages will continue to thirst; the deep, sinful problems will remain; and we will grow tired, thirsty, and ready to give up or give in to temptations—whatever appeals to our desires in the moment. All too often Ryan and I receive a message from a husband or wife asking for prayer for their marriage when they have tried to quench their thirst through something or someone else other than God, and sin has destroyed them. The common thread we see in each of these stories is a hardening of hearts, both toward God and each other. More often than not this leads to one or both spouses looking elsewhere for their needs to be met. The result is typically an affair (emotional or physical) or an addiction (pornography, substance abuse, or secret financial debt).

Sin devastates for generations, but God is gracious and loving enough to bring deep healing. He doesn't necessarily remove the pain but he shows us how sovereign and present he is in the midst of brokenness. He's done that in my own life. Having come from a divorced home, I know firsthand what it means to struggle with trust. But God is so good to point me back to him, and my gratefulness toward him and my husband have only grown. I can honestly say that I wouldn't be the person and wife I am today without those hardships.

Thirst quenching feels like a cycle: we receive help, guidance, love, and instruction from the Holy Spirit; our thirst is quenched! We are working diligently to follow the Holy Spirit's guidance. But before we know it, we take the reins again—and the temptation for control begins. One temptation we have found to be common is the pull to get our priorities out of order.

FOR REFLECTION

- Prior to reading this chapter, how did you and your spouse define love?
- How has understanding God's love for you (and your spouse) challenged your previous view of love?
- How can you love your spouse more selflessly?
- Identify one or two areas where your marriage is "thirsty" and in need of more love.

5

Time and Priorities

What Being Christ-Centered Truly Means

In necessary things, unity; in doubtful things,
liberty; in all things, charity.

Richard Baxter

About a year after Ryan and I returned from our Swiss adventure, I started at an engineering firm as a marketing coordinator when the industry was booming. It was a shiny start to my new career. I made quick work of acquiring new contracts, keeping our engineers working, helping the company thrive, and adding feathers to my boss's cap. Everyone was winning. However, when the market crashed and construction came to a screeching halt, everything changed. Being the emotional person that I am, I found this devastating. I had so much anxiety that I would get up at 5:00 a.m. to work out at the gym to help relieve my anxiousness. After that I would work a full day and then head out to the barn for a post-work ride on my horse. I looked everywhere for rest and relief except to the One who has an abundance of otherworldly peace. Ryan and I constantly felt like we were questioning our decisions about work, home, and finances—our priorities felt right, but everything was just on the verge of chaos. Not a fun place to live.

Then, one February, everything changed. Ryan found a crazy deal on flights to Munich, so he bought them as a Valentine's Day gift and surprised me with an eighteen-day backpacking trip through Europe. This was about three years after our first Switzerland adventure, so we were both excited for a less surgical experience this time. I'm a quality time person, so I was very much looking forward to one-on-one time with Ryan—lots of uninterrupted, intimate, fifteen-hour-train-ride, walking-everywhere-with-zero-distractions quality time. It was during this time together that God began to break down our walls and recalibrate our hearts and minds. During our trip it became painfully obvious how little time we spent together and how our relationship lacked depth and purpose. Our marriage was tired. *We* were tired and unsettled. Ryan felt a check in his heart that prompted hard conversations about our priorities. We realized that good things had taken up too much of our heart-space, and while fruit was being produced in other areas, our marriage was stagnant and simply existing. We were spread so thin that our marriage lacked joy and peace. I remember thinking, *God didn't create us to live like this. This isn't his best for intimacy with each other, or with him.* We desperately needed margin—room for each other—and we needed to reset our priorities. We were a mess on many levels, and this trip opened our eyes to finally see that.

One conversation in particular marks one of the most significant pivot points in our marriage. Ryan said, "At the end of my life, when I'm standing before God, I'll give an account to him for my family and how I led them. *I don't want this to be the account I give.*" From then on, the world we had formed—good-paying jobs, intense level of church involvement, my time with horses—all began to crumble. We didn't know what the future would hold, but we knew the present wasn't really what God wanted for our marriage, our family, or this life he had given us.

Good Things Gone Bad

The most frustrating part of this process was that everything that had gotten us to that point was good! Our mistaken identities turned good things sour. Like Eve in the garden, we fell for the lie that we could be our own gods—masters of own destinies. It started subtly, but we had found our identities in the wrong places and put our security in the wrong things. We hammered God's good provision into idols as we looked to them for life and meaning that only Christ can give.

Sometimes we need to walk away from good things to reset our hearts on Christ and his eternal work. For Ryan and me, walking away was extremely hard. It took many painful, necessary conversations and, unfortunately, a few severed relationships. But God's gracious hand guided our every step. He knew the only way for us to walk away was to *move away*. We thought we were following our own business goals, but God was luring us south. He was leading us toward true reliance on him and away from familiarity and false security.

Thus began our journey to the desert, both figuratively and literally. In August of that year, just six months after our European epiphany, we packed up our life and drove south to our new home: Palm Desert, California.

Our time in the desert was one of deep and true healing for our souls and our relationship. It was a time of reconciliation with God and each other. The desert was a time of new beginnings. We began experiencing real change that could only have come from Jesus. Digging deep for the living water our souls were so thirsty for, I felt like my walk with the Lord became newer and truer. From the time we arrived in California, God began rebuilding all that had been crushed. He was making all things new—and it took him moving us out of the lush, green land of the northwest and placing us in a dry, barren desert valley for us to see it. As we now realize, the spiritual parallels were far more significant than we could have ever imagined.

A Common Conundrum

RYAN

Selena and I could never have anticipated the work God started during our time in the desert. One of the clearest works he began was reorienting our hearts on what matters most.

Keeping our priorities in check is a constant struggle—one I imagine will last our entire lives. Busyness is an eager guest in the Frederick household, and on top of that, technology would gladly soak up every spare moment. If we're not mindful, we can easily scroll, tap, and flick aimlessly through social media feeds on our phones instead of engaging with each other and our children.

I'm convinced that when our generation grows old we'll wish we'd spent fewer hours staring at screens. We'll look back on our lives and wonder what could have been if we had not incessantly checked our devices or been so eagerly entertained. We will remember and cherish the face-to-face moments we spent with those we love. We will value every instance we pressed into real life, through the good and the bad. We will appreciate the meals and conversations we had when our focus was undivided and unshared—uncaptured by our smartphones or anything other than memory. We will reminisce about wrestling with God, forging into his Word, and dealing with difficult issues of our faith in Christ.

When we're old we will finally recognize distractions for what they truly and tragically are: noisy interruptions to the beautiful music of raw—*real*—life.

It's one of God's amazing graces to make us aware of wrong priorities and fleeting distractions before we regret them. As I write this, I'm thankful. I'm thankful to be thinking about priorities, thankful that you're here to process alongside me. As we venture further, rest in Christ and know that the Holy Spirit is molding your heart to align your priorities with God's. Maintaining godly priorities is a central issue for your marriage. If you're not intentional about centering your life on Christ, your priorities will jump out of order. Disordering is often subtle and gradual and, as in our case, usually caused by *good* things turned *bad*.

Church involvement is good, but over-volunteering will stretch you too thin and dilute your effectiveness. Working is great, but too much work steals from quality time with your spouse and family. Technology is an amazing tool, but too much of it robs from real life. When your priorities are out of order, you will feel it. We feel it when we begin to bicker and argue over small things as our patience runs dry. If I overwork, Selena's appreciation of my provision transforms into resentment of whatever I'm doing or, worse yet, of me as her husband.

Your priorities are the greatest indicators of what—or *who*—you love most. And like all sin, wrong priorities will wreak havoc in your life and marriage.

The most common byproducts of misplaced priorities in marriage are a lack of quality time, a steady degradation of communication, and the slow distancing of spouses from one another. Their intimacy suffers as the gap between them widens, and eventually something—someone—has to give.

The List

My dad (we'll call him Dr. Frederick) is a psychologist who has helped countless husbands and wives throughout decades of running his counseling practice. Among all the married couples who have gone to him for help, time and priorities are by far the most common causes for marital strife, separation, and divorce.

The advent of the internet has produced new opportunities for skewed priorities. Dr. Frederick has a unique perspective, having counseled couples on either side of the information age—both pre- and post-internet. He's observed troubled marriages closely over the past thirty years and found that while the sources of distraction have evolved, the core issues remain unchanged: misplaced priorities and being too busy—too preoccupied. Couples don't have time for each other. They don't make room or time for their marriages to flourish.

We've all heard the phrase, "You make time for what's important." It's true. Look at how you spend your time and you will see what's most important to you.

Right priorities are neat and easy to articulate on paper, but reality is full of gray areas. Hierarchical lists like the one below look ideal, but they easily break down during daily life. Our functional priorities—the ones we actually live—are often a response to who's loudest and what's most urgent instead of who or what is most *important*. Your ideal list of priorities probably looks like this:

Priority 1 God

Priority 2 Spouse

Priority 3 Kids

Priority 4 Others

The above hierarchy is good. It's even biblically sound. It reflects, to an extent, what God's Word says about priorities:

> You shall love the Lord your God with all your heart and with all your soul and with all your mind. This is the great and first commandment. And a second is like it: You shall love your neighbor as yourself. On these two commandments depend all the Law and the Prophets. (Matt. 22:37–40)

This passage appears to apply perfectly to our ideal priority list. First, love God. Next, love others. It fits!

However (tell me you didn't see this coming), why do we still fail at keeping God first? Why do so many days look like this: wake up, check your phone, rush out the door, return from work, watch TV, go to bed, repeat—all without uttering a single prayer or reading even one passage from God's Word? You may hit the mark a few days a week, or perhaps you can succeed most days with the help of above-average willpower. However, if you're like most, you won't always make time for what's important.

The Problem with the List

Sequentially listing our God-given priorities is a Western response to Christ's calling. Western culture is task-oriented; we're inclined to read that Matthew 22 passage as a to-do list. That being the case, a successful day likely looks like this: wake up, pray, and have devotions (*love God, check*). Treat others well by speaking kindly, sharing the gospel, or giving of your time and money (*love others, double check*). Move on to the next item.

I'm oversimplifying, but you get the point. A hierarchical list compels us to check items off instead of living out God's priorities with our whole being. I don't believe a top-down approach is our best response to Jesus's powerful, weighty statements.

Take a moment and read the above passage again. Notice the emphasis placed on *all* of you. The Greek word for all is literally translated as "whole" (*holē*). Is it possible to love God with our *whole* selves and still have some left over for others? Not really. The instant I break from loving God actively and start loving others, I stop giving him *all* of me, right? Not to worry—Jesus wasn't setting us up for failure.

God is not just first; he *is*. Consider his magnitude. He holds the entire universe in his hands. He keeps countless atomic particles humming around in perfect order while, at the same time, binding galaxies together and taming the hottest stars. He *is* in every time, in every place. As Paul wrote, "in him all things hold together" (Col. 1:17). He is unmatched and uninhibited; a consuming fire, Lord of hosts, ruler of all.

God is not merely first on our priority list; he *is* the list. Without him, everything falls apart. Everything becomes nothing without God's intimate involvement.

Jesus didn't simply delegate tasks from heaven like a divine office memo. Jesus is calling you to be *consumed* by God, to be captivated by him—totally satisfied but forever longing for more. Jesus's call to love God with *all* your heart is the antithesis of distraction and it obliterates Christian to-dos. To a person who trusts Jesus, nothing matters more than him but everything else matters more than before *because* of him.

In marriage, instead of putting each other on our to-do lists, we are called to love one another as we are consumed with God from the inside out. Marital priorities fall into their right places as we establish our love in Christ. Then our priorities transform from being a top-down list to something more like concentric circles. Everything we do radiates outward from the center, our identity in Christ. If ever our priorities are out of place, we need only look to Christ, repent, and allow his grace to wash over us and reorient our lives by the power of the gospel.

In lieu of a priority list, let's explore a concentric view that we've found sustainable and enriching for our life and marriage.

Gospel Priorities: The Concentric View

Godly priorities don't just start with Christ, they're *centered* on him. Everything that matters to him matters to you. It's

97

cause and effect. Your marriage matters. Your spouse matters. Discipleship matters. People matter.

Priority Circle #1: Seek God and His Kingdom

God wants to be the central pursuit in our lives. Then, his kingdom. Everything radiates outward from him. Our priorities get mixed up when we forget who God is and what he has promised. We may work more because we're afraid of lack. We may overcommit to *good* activities because, at our core, we are trying to convince ourselves that we're worthy of God's love or that our identity is secure. If we're motivated by fear—any anxiety caused by disbelieving the gospel—we miss God's call to cherish and trust him above all else.

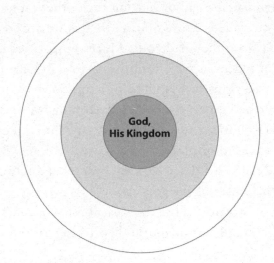

Jesus tells his disciples,

Therefore do not be anxious, saying, "What shall we eat?" or "What shall we drink?" or "What shall we wear?" For the Gentiles seek after all these things, and your heavenly Father knows that you need them all. But seek first the kingdom of

God and his righteousness, and all these things will be added to you. (Matt. 6:31–33)

The above passage is a call to *rest* in God's sufficiency—his sovereignty. His kingdom and his righteousness are sure! *Seeking God's kingdom and his righteousness* forces us to turn our gaze—our focus and our priorities—to God. We trust in his character, his promises, and his redemption. This is the most loving command we could possibly receive, as it centers our entire existence on God himself. In him, we have purpose, reason to love, and cause to forgive. We have context for every aspect of life, and our priorities radiate outward from a heart *consumed* by God. But what does it mean to be consumed by him?

Being consumed by God means *experiencing* and *knowing* him. Reading his Word and communing with him through prayer and worship are vital to your relationship with God and each other, and that vitality should be reflected in your priorities. As you read the Bible, let its words bear weight in your life. Let Christ define who you are as you experience grace and forgiveness. Wrestle with Scripture and digest it. Internalize it and ask hard questions. Seek wisdom within your Bible's pages and apply what it says. Our God has faithfully revealed himself through his Word, and when we read it we encounter him.

And when we encounter God through his Word we respond with prayer. Praying is richest when grounded in what God has already said. Just as knowing each other intimately in marriage requires communication, so does your relationship with God. As you pray, allow time and space for the Holy Spirit to speak, listen when he does, and respond.

Finally, Bible study and prayer should incite awe, wonder, and worship. God's goodness, holiness, and justice are overwhelming; indeed, we *should* be overwhelmed: he's God! We are human sinners saved by grace, limited in our scope, capacity, and understanding. Yet God has lovingly granted us access to him through the person and work of Christ. He has gifted us his Word and the Holy Spirit. He has proven over and over again his faithfulness, sovereignty, and power. What else can we *do* but worship him? Complete worship is the only human response to encountering the person of God.

Making time to encounter God takes intentionality. One of the most profound practices we've discovered is daily family worship. The idea is simple and definitely not new: read Scripture, sing a song (usually "Jesus Loves Me" or something similar), and pray together every day as a family. For Selena and me, this is in addition to our personal devotional times with God; for our kids, it's a beautiful (albeit brief) exercise in prioritizing worship. It takes us five minutes around the breakfast table but the impact is eternal.[1]

Every aspect of how we love each other in marriage radiates outward from this first priority circle—our central pursuit—the God of the universe. He is the ultimate prize, both the reason and the means to love each other well, which is the next priority circle.

Priority Circle #2: Love Neighbors and Make Disciples

With God firmly at the center, we are endowed with the freedom, joy, and glad privilege of being Christ's active ambassadors here on earth. We do this by loving others and making disciples, starting with our spouses and children.

Jesus's next and final command—our second priority circle—is to "love your neighbor as yourself" (Mark 12:31).

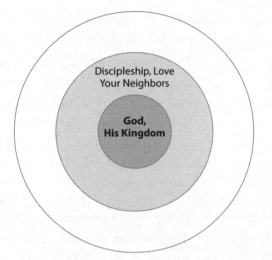

We often read "neighbor" to mean *everyone besides God* in an abstract sense. While that is true, we lose the truer meaning when we oversimplify.

We live in a neighborhood with 170 homes. It can be said that anyone within its boundary is our neighbor. The same goes for anyone living in our city. But no one is more our neighbor than the people living next door. We see them often, know them by name, and interact regularly. We have real relationship with them.

The farther we venture away from our home and daily lives, the more abstract *neighbor* becomes. I don't believe Jesus was being abstract when he commanded us to love our neighbors. He was being practical—concrete. He was commanding us to love people in general, yes, but it must start with those closest to home. And who lives closer to home than those *in* our home? Fulfilling Jesus's command to love our neighbors begins with our closest neighbors of all: our spouses and kids. It starts with love, but it doesn't stop there.

Loving our spouses well is not without ambition. There is a clear goal in mind, which we find in the Great Commission:

> And Jesus came and said to them, "All authority in heaven and on earth has been given to me. Go therefore and make disciples of all nations, baptizing them in the name of the Father and of the Son and of the Holy Spirit, teaching them to observe all that I have commanded you. And behold, I am with you always, to the end of the age." (Matt. 28:18–20)

Our greatest reason for loving one another in marriage is to make disciples of each other and our children. In marriage, husband and wife are called to love each other first and best. This means fiercely guarding our marriage from activities, people, and distractions that chip away at our intimacy and unity. For us, guarding our marriage meant some good things had to go.

When Selena and I began understanding this aspect of our call as husband and wife, we naturally identified good things that had gone bad in our marriage. I stopped volunteering at church for a time. Selena sold her horse. Both were good activities that had become poisonous for our marriage and contrary to Christ's call to love and disciple each other. How can we love and minister to others honestly (or effectively) if the very act of doing so hurts those we are called to love and minister to first? Why else are elders called to manage "their children and their own households well" (1 Tim. 3:12) before leading the church? Clearly hearing your call to love your spouse and kids first makes wrong priorities clear. If anything hinders loving your family well or stifles discipleship within your family, it must be eliminated. Period. It's a tough truth to grasp but is vital for a healthy, thriving marriage.

As you read this, consider what priorities may be out of place in your life. Having a job is good; we are called to work diligently and glorify God in the process. But what if the very job that puts food on your table keeps you from spending time sitting around it together? Ministry is good; we are called to serve and help others through the local church. However, is it right to give your best hours to others if your absence makes your spouse feel disconnected, unimportant, and resentful?

This was a pivotal realization for me: there are seasons when intense work or ministry is required, but all seasons must end. When I was starting our business, I worked eighty hours per week. It taxed us immensely, but it's over. I now work about thirty hours per week; if it takes longer it's not important. Busy seasons are part of life, but always put a timeline on them to preserve the health of your marriage. Years of winter will freeze even the warmest homes, empty the fullest tables, and extinguish the strongest fires.

Keep God at the center, then love your neighbors and make disciples. Your closest, first neighbors are your spouse and kids. From there, your ministry will naturally extend outward to those in your community and "to the ends of the earth."

Priority Circle #3: Enjoy God's Grace, Give Him Glory

The third and outermost priority circle is our catchall for everything else. It's simply this: enjoy God's grace, give him glory. When the dust settles, what's the point? We fight and strive to maintain godly priorities—to apply wisdom—but

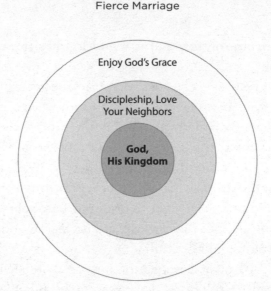

to what end? The final circle helps answer that question by reminding us to *be* and to enjoy the graces of God, for his ultimate glory. It's a reminder to rest in God's sovereignty.

Our best example comes from the book of Ecclesiastes. Its author, Solomon, was one of the wealthiest people in history and was lauded for his unmatched wisdom. He is one of my favorite biblical authors—as you read his words, you can feel his emotional rawness. Whether he's writing about love or weighing his very existence, he holds nothing back. His biblical works range from poetic romance (Song of Solomon) to pragmatic advice (Proverbs) and venting existential frustration (Ecclesiastes). Exactly my cup of tea!

My favorite book by Solomon is Ecclesiastes. It's chock-full of unfiltered contemplation—a collection of thoughts that seem to have been hurriedly scribbled down in moments of frustration. It's as if Solomon is throwing up his hands and shouting, "What's the point?" He writes,

And I applied my heart to know wisdom and to know madness and folly. I perceived that this also is but a striving after the wind.

> For in much wisdom is much vexation,
>> and he who increases knowledge increases sorrow.
>> (Eccles. 1:17–18)

I can relate; perhaps you can too.

The entire book carries a melancholy tone, but I believe it's primarily a book about sweet surrender—about reaching the end of ambition and being reminded to simply *be*, to enjoy life, and to trust God. You can sense Solomon's existential frustration wax and wane, almost like music. It's tense, but you feel his relief when he quietly resigns himself to God's sovereignty over and over again.

> Go, eat your bread with joy, and drink your wine with a merry heart, for God has already approved what you do. . . .
>> Enjoy life with the wife whom you love, all the days of your vain life that he has given you under the sun, because that is your portion in life and in your toil at which you toil under the sun. Whatever your hand finds to do, do it with your might. (Eccles. 9:7, 9–10)

This passage is where we get our third priority circle. It's our reminder to relax and enjoy God's grace over our lives—to quit *doing* and start *being*.

We can get so focused on *doing* that we forget to simply *be*. Just being together is medicine to your marriage; it's necessary and irreplaceable for the health of your relationship. There is always more gospel work to do, but thank God that it's his master work, not yours. Extra blessings in life are good gifts from God and they are to be enjoyed here, now. With Christ at the center, you are free to rest (trust) in his sovereignty, free from pressure to strive for more for its own sake.

As Selena mentioned, she enjoys riding horses. She struggled with guilt for a long time because of the expense it placed on our family's finances and time. Some of what she felt was conviction because of misplaced priorities, but much of it was just plain guilt. She felt bad for reasons unrelated to her personal walk with God or the health of our marriage. It's taken years for us to realize that extra blessings like horses (or running water, for that matter) are to be enjoyed in the context of God's goodness—because *he has allowed it*. Doing so fulfills our highest calling as children of God: to enjoy him and to give him glory in our enjoyment.

Aside from indulgence, you are free to enjoy unmerited, even illogical gifts from God. They are vain joys in themselves—which is Solomon's repeated conclusion—but as gifts from God, good enjoyments are chock-full of eternal purpose. You are free to *be*, and to "eat your bread with joy, and drink your wine with a merry heart, for God has already approved what you do" (Eccles. 9:7).

When God finished creation, he called it good and he rested. Eden was human existence as God intended—without sin, humankind in perfect relationship with him and enjoying his good creation. Adam and Eve were placed in the garden to simply exist—to *be*. When God's work is done on the final day, he will redeem creation and restore perfection. We will once again *be* in perfect relationship with God, enjoy his grace, and give him eternal glory.

Our lives in Christ today—here and now—can be a glimpse of eternity. We are called to enjoy the grace of God in Christ and glorify him through our worship. Jesus encourages his disciples by reminding them that he is their vine—their source of life and nourishment—and they are the branches. They are reminded to "abide" in him by resting in and enjoying the grace of God, remembering him as their only source for sustenance and fulfillment:

> Already you are clean because of the word that I have spoken to you. Abide in me, and I in you. As the branch cannot bear fruit by itself, unless it abides in the vine, neither can you, unless you abide in me. I am the vine; you are the branches. Whoever abides in me and I in him, he it is that bears much fruit, for apart from me you can do nothing. (John 15:3–5)

Abide in Christ. *Be* in him. He alone will produce fruit in your life. And as you abide, enjoy the journey. When you are in Christ, you are in God's family. God lavishes gifts on his children like the loving Father that he is. He gives to you for your enjoyment, for your pleasure. Rest in God's sovereignty, savor every good moment, and do so in the context of his eternal, unending, illogical grace.

Establishing healthy, God-centered priorities is the beginning of establishing health in other key areas of your marriage. So much marital frustration can be avoided if both spouses are simply available for quality communication instead of being too busy.

Over-busyness is a rampant problem in our culture. Fight it. Fight for rest. And fight for margin. Fight to create the extra space you need in your marriage to truly connect and have real conversation. Then, once you've learned to communicate well, you can talk through everything. In fact, communication is exactly what we'll be exploring next.

FOR REFLECTION

- How can the concentric view of priorities challenge the way you and your spouse prioritize?
- Are there areas in your life that need pruning? Why?
- Discuss with your spouse what this pruning will look like.

6

Communication and Connection

Using Your Words to Strengthen Your Marriage

> When people talk, listen completely. Most people
> never listen.
>
> Ernest Hemingway

The day I turned sixteen I couldn't wait to get my driver's license. Most of my friends at school—namely, Selena—were already driving, so I couldn't wait to join them. Seeing my excitement, my parents took me to the licensing office as soon as it opened so I could take my test. By the time we arrived, my excitement turned to anxiety as I grasped the stakes. If I failed the test, my dreams of freedom would be shattered. If I passed, my life would be forever changed for the better. I even had plans to celebrate with friends later that evening, and Selena was going to be there (we weren't dating yet). I was so sure I would pass—why not make plans? This was before the anxiety set in, of course.

I nervously took the driver's seat as the examiner watched and noted my every move. Seat belt, check. Rearview mirror, check. Side mirrors, good to go.

I gave myself a pep talk. *You got this, just don't choke. Remember your training.*

It was almost like I was getting ready to contend for a heavyweight title. I had studied for months and driven with my parents as much as humanly possible. All I had to do was keep my cool. Which I did—for the most part.

I aced every aspect of the test. I backed around corners like a swan taking flight. I parallel parked like a ninja. I observed all speed limits, merged with poise, and checked blind spots like I had been driving for decades. Just as the test was coming to a close, we rounded the last corner, and I could see the licensing office just ahead. Just one more intersection to go. *I'm gonna make it!* I thought to myself. *Victory is mine!*

Then it happened.

Just as I approached the last intersection, the green light turned yellow. Except it wasn't one of those times when the choice to stop or go was clear. It was an awkward yellow. There wasn't enough space to stop without slamming on the brakes, but I wasn't so close that I knew for sure I'd make it through the intersection before it turned red.

Oh, no. My stomach dropped. I knew I was at a literal and a figurative crossroads! This was the single moment that would decide my destiny.

Time slowed to a crawl. The hair on my neck stood on end. I white-knuckled ten and two as my brain flooded with gallons of every hormone that causes teenage boys to go instantly idiotic. In a flash, I made my choice—there was no going back. I *slammed* on the gas pedal. My instructor grabbed his above-window handle, locked his knees, pushed his feet firmly into the floor, and flattened his head and back against his seat. I wondered if he heard the tires scrape against the wheel wells as I bottomed out the shocks on my '94 Honda Civic and bounced through the intersection. I caught a glimpse of the yellow light as it changed to red before immediately applying heavy pressure to the brake and turning hard into the licensing office.

I sheepishly pulled into the closest drive test parking stall. My instructor scribbled something on his clipboard. I put the car in park and let it idle, but my heart still raced at the speed of awkward yellow.

Pregnant pause. Long silence. I could hear my examiner catching his breath.

"How did I d—" I started to say.

"You failed," he interrupted. "You can't run a red light and expect to pass your driver's test."

In an instant I was doomed to a life filled with bicycles and bus stops. I burned through the stages of grief faster than you can say "eight-ball shifter." I blasted past denial and anger before making a pit stop at bargaining. The examiner wouldn't have it. So I cut my losses and went home to get started on depression. I didn't hit acceptance until a few days later—just in time to retake my driver's test.

Seeing the Signals

Communication is all about signals. You send and receive signals through your words, body language, tone, and timing to relay information. The information you send is powerful because it deeply affects your relationship—your sense of safety, trust, and emotional intimacy. It's helpful to recall the purpose of traffic lights. Their sole function is to enable communication between vehicles on the road. Green tells drivers it's safe to drive through an intersection because the cross traffic has a red light and should be stopped. This agreed method of communication allows traffic to function harmoniously, assuming all drivers recognize and honor the same system. If you run a red light—if you miss the signal—you're likely to cause a collision.

The same is true for communication in marriage. If you miss the signals your spouse is sending, or send the wrong ones yourself, you may be headed for a collision. If and when your signals are in sync, you'll experience harmony, safety, and freedom.

A Direct Line to the Heart

God created everything by his words, and Jesus is called the Living Word. Words are important—they were designed that way! Also, Scripture is full of verses warning against foolish talk and refusing to listen.

The effects of good and bad communication are magnified in marriage because of how close you are to one another. You share unprecedented access to each other's hearts. Your words, if misused, can cause damage. But they can also bring healing.

The verse below represents a prevalent theme throughout Scripture:

> There is one whose rash words are like sword
>   thrusts,
>   but the tongue of the wise brings healing. (Prov.
>   12:18)

My heart surgeon intentionally left four wires in my chest when they closed me up. Each one was tied off and sewn to my skin just below my rib cage in two rows of two. I remember looking down and thinking about how weird they looked, and I still have the scars to remind me. Each wire entered into my chest, looped under my ribs, and traced upward to touch a strategic place on my heart. Their sole purpose was to provide my doctors with direct access in case they needed to restart my heart during the week following my surgery. If my heart stopped beating, they literally had the power to bring me back to life. They also had the ability to kill me in an instant—but I try not to focus on that. (By the way, when they pulled them out I was fully conscious. It was horrible, but it makes for a great story.)

You have a direct line to your spouse's heart. Your words can give life or they can bring death. This is true for words in general. "Death and life are in the power of the tongue, and those who love it will eat its fruits" (18:21). How much more powerful are the words exchanged between spouses? How much more careful should we be in how we communicate with each other?

The goal in communication is always to advance your relationship and enhance your intimacy. Yes, you will need to discuss daily tasks and mundane life to-dos, but even benign conversations can either help or hurt your overall communication climate and relational intimacy. It's crucial to recognize common communication pitfalls so you can steer clear.

In the next section, Selena will discuss how to understand and recover from communication breakdowns, then I'll return to explore practical ideas for gospel-fueled, marriage-strengthening communication.

Dealing with Breakdowns

SELENA

Our fleshly reactions are always rooted in some functional disbelief in the gospel. You'll never communicate more poorly than when being right becomes integral to your identity, when feeling disrespected is an assault on your worth, and when fixing injustice is your sole responsibility. Remembering the sufficiency of Christ in hard moments changes everything. It's crucial and challenging to remember that we are secure in God, our worth is rooted in God's love (which was proven on the cross), and fixing injustice is God's domain. This is right about where the sanctifying work of marriage begins to dig in. Learning to communicate is perhaps the most obvious and consistent area where Ryan and I feel the heat of God's sanctification hard at work, and it is a slow, arduous, *necessary* process. There's always fire involved in refining. Our fieriest moments typically happen when our pride and selfishness are in full force.

In communicating with your spouse, you will sometimes feel like your identity is under attack. You will feel like you're being disrespected. And you will feel a need for justice. You will need to forgive and you will need to be forgiven. You will need grace and you will need to extend it. Speaking from personal experience, communication will reveal your need for Jesus without fail. It will also expose God's continuous work in your hearts and provide a plethora of opportunities to minister to each other.

Ryan has a direct line to my heart, and it makes our communication both sacred and challenging. His words (or lack thereof) carry more weight because he is my husband. I'm convinced that communication is a sanctifying cycle in which the words we speak highlight the issues of our hearts (Luke 6:45). Breakdowns in communication are inevitable. It's in these breakdowns that we can experience and extend God's grace by understanding that the goal is reconciliation and not simply being "right." Reconciling requires us to listen and hear, to engage and understand, remembering that we are no better than our spouse but we are all saved and loved by God's grace.

More Than Words

Ryan's one responsibility in the morning is to take the garbage out (if it wasn't taken out the night before). It's a point of contention for us because I don't want to nag him, but if I don't remind him, he tends to forget. One morning, after Ryan got home from the gym, I politely asked him to please take out the garbage (we'd had fish for dinner the night before and it was beginning to stink). He said he would. Lunch rolled around, the fish smell was at an all-time high. He came downstairs for lunch (he works from home). I looked at him and I looked at the garbage; no exchange of words. It was now time for dinner, and the stench was beyond grotesque. *Again* he came downstairs; I looked at him and looked at the garbage. Our looks and bodies squared off a bit. He got frustrated and began explaining all the reasons why he *would* take it out. Could I have taken the garbage out? Yes, but for me it was the principle. He said he would take out the garbage but apparently didn't indicate *when*, just that he would at some point that day.

Now I'm not trying to paint him in a bad light, because I'm incredibly grateful for everything he does for our family. But I'm sure if you reflect on your own marriage, you can see how communication breakdowns can begin. A small disagreement or frustration with your spouse in the morning, a complete lack of words (or texts) to each other *all* day, and yet you both know (and *feel*) exactly what is being communicated. The feelings of anger and frustration are obvious, making our silent spells anything but golden.

On the flipside, we also have days when we talk and interact all day but it does nothing to build our closeness. Although we are communicating with each other, it feels incredibly shallow, and we both feel disconnected and annoyed. Needless to say, communication is more than the words we share; it's a telltale sign of what's going on in our hearts and the real focus of our souls.

In our case, I was frustrated with Ryan for not taking out the garbage even though he said he would. In an attempt to not nag him, I left the stinky garbage in the bin—one small task. *Does he even know what I do during the day?* Obviously my issue was not the garbage; it was that I selfishly felt like I was doing more around the house than he was. Hmm, keeping track of wrongs much?

Breakdown To-Dos

When our communication begins to break down, my tendency is to see how I can fix it rather than first going to God's

Word (that should be hidden in my heart) and humbly seeking his instruction. James 1:19–22 provides clear framework for us in this instance:

> Know this, my beloved brothers: let every person be quick to hear, slow to speak, slow to anger; for the anger of man does not produce the righteousness of God. Therefore put away all filthiness and rampant wickedness and receive with meekness the implanted word, which is able to save your souls.
>
> But be doers of the word, and not hearers only, deceiving yourselves.

If we break down this passage of Scripture, James offers us four instructions.

1. Be Quick to Hear

Listen for what the real issue is. In the case of the stinky fish garbage, I didn't once think to ask Ryan if he was having a busy day and needed my help. I didn't notice how quickly he was on the phone for a meeting, or how his tone seemed a little overwhelmed when we talked about the garbage. Hearing requires the attention of the ears and the heart. When I hear what is going on in my husband's world, my heart is stirred to love him. When I hear my husband's heart—not just his words—it helps me see him as the gift he is and remember how (like me) he's a work in progress. It's not about keeping score but about extending grace and recognizing an opportunity to show him covenant love, despite my own feelings or whatever craziness has happened in my day.

When you listen to your spouse, you're saying to them, "I care about you and I value what you're saying. I want to give you my mind, my time, and my undivided attention." When you're listening, you're loving. Listening is all about respect. When you listen to your spouse you are affirming them by telling them they are valuable and worth your full engagement. Disrespect is the dark underbelly of familiarity. As you grow closer to each other (good!) it's easy to express your familiarity in ways that are actually disrespectful (bad!).

We've discovered three ways this plays out in our communication: distractions, interruptions, and failure to empathize. Listening never needed to be more intentional than now. We live in a time riddled with distraction opportunities. Every phone bing, buzz, bleep, tweet, and notification would love to steal a few seconds of our time. Add that to the sense of intrigue and validation offered on social media, and we've got a recipe for diluted, shortened attention.

Most poor communication in our marriage starts with one of us being disengaged and looking down at our phone. Talking gets frustrating because someone isn't really paying attention; one of us isn't listening. It's not as if Ryan checks his email while I'm bawling my eyes out; it's never that drastic. The timing usually seems harmless. But if distraction is a common enough theme, disengagement evolves into disconnection. The thing about distraction is that it's never as harmless as it seems. It's actually a subtle form of disrespect. When I'm consistently distracted during conversations, I am functionally saying to my spouse, "This other thing is more important than you." Few would say that with their words, but actions and body language speak truth as clearly.

Another enemy of listening is interruption. Interrupting inhibits listening and stops dialogue in its tracks. I hate to admit it, but I interrupt *way* too much. My excitement or ability to relate takes over, I begin thinking about what I want to say, and then—poof—interruption. Then Ryan forgets his thought and usually gets annoyed. I don't do it intentionally, but I've come to realize that I interrupt because I don't really want to know what Ryan is going to say. I either assume I know where he's going, I stop caring about it (he explains things with too much detail sometimes), or I get too eager to say what I'm thinking. Regardless of my reasons for interrupting, I really want Ryan to know he is loved, and one way I can show him is by listening.

Remember, we have direct lines to each other's hearts. When we fail to listen to each other, we fail to respect each other. Listening is an active opening of our hearts and minds, and in that it's an act of generosity. Communication is impossible without our intentional attention to one another. So shove distractions aside, keep interruptions at bay, and seek to understand *before* being understood.

2. Be Slow to Speak

Admittedly, too many of my quick nagging looks or remarks (as in the case of the stinky fish garbage) have escaped me. I failed to mention that while Ryan wasn't taking out the garbage, I was downstairs stewing. Stewing about the list in my mind that justified why I *should not* have to take out the garbage. Ryan often teases me about how articulate I can be when I'm angry. I'm quick to break out the full arsenal of sharp words, short responses, the coldest of shoulders, and of course, every wife's secret weapon: *the look*. I tend to wear my heart on my sleeve, and if I'm feeling something (anger), it's hard for me not to act on it. Needless to say, being slow to speak is a hard thing for me. Too many times

I sit there "listening" to Ryan, but in my mind I'm thinking about what *I* need to say.

Being slow to speak means putting our words through another filter, the filter of time. I may not have said anything aloud to Ryan, but I communicated a lot through my look. I failed to listen and hear *all of Ryan*, which made me quick to judge and communicate my prideful and selfish sense of injustice rather than love and grace. James 3:4–5 reminds me of the power of the tongue and the importance of being slow to speak:

> Look at the ships also: though they are so large and are driven by strong winds, they are guided by a very small rudder wherever the will of the pilot directs. So also the tongue is a small member, yet it boasts of great things.

How we listen is crucial, but so is how we speak. Wise talking is knowing when to speak as much as when to pause. I'm a verbal processor and I have no trouble putting words out there—especially when I feel passionately. The downside is that though my words are plentiful, they're not always productive. They can be said in haste and convey meaning I don't intend.

Ryan, however, isn't a natural talker. He's always been an internal processor. I can't tell you how many times I've been talking to him and he says nothing in spots where I implicitly expect his feedback. After about ten minutes of what feels like a one-way conversation, I'll ask him, "Are you even listening to me?" Knowing how this frustrates me, he'll usually respond with, "Sorry, I've been responding to you in my head. Here's what I'm thinking . . ." We can both improve on speaking intentionally, for entirely different reasons.

I want so badly to be heard and understood, but sometimes I can't articulate exactly what I'm feeling in the moment so I'll just start throwing sentences out there. I've realized that I need time to pause and rest before speaking. I need time to process my response. Perhaps that's what James is talking about. He is saying that we must remain levelheaded and intentional in how we interact with each other. It is good to pause and think things through! How many times have you gotten yourself into trouble by reacting too quickly? Personally, I've lost count. But I'm learning.

Being "slow to speak" isn't the same as saying "don't ever speak." This is where internal processors can learn to improve. Marriage involves lots and lots of dialogue. If one of you is inclined to few words, this can default to too little communication and make life difficult for the other person. Steady discourse between both spouses is crucial to connection. If you're the quiet one, learn to express how you're feeling and thinking. Doing so gives your spouse two opportunities: to know you more deeply and to help you through his or her gifts. Ryan has said many times, "Why didn't I ask for your input sooner? I could have saved weeks!" In marriage, both husband and wife bring different, complementary perspectives and spiritual gifts. By engaging in intentional conversation (even when it seems unnatural), you acknowledge your need for each other's help.

3. Be Slow to Anger

One evening we were driving home from our community group (church small group), and I was in a mood. Ryan and I were arguing about something he had said to me in front of people. It had made me feel embarrassed, though in reality it wasn't awkward or weird at all. I was mad as a hornet and his response revealed undealt-with sin in my heart. In his patient and loving way, he said, "You know you don't have to respond out of anger? There are other ways you can respond, even if you are angry." Ugh, he was right. My angry response came from my short fuse. Being slow to anger lengthens the fuse and allows me to process my feelings and the motivations behind them. In other words, by being slow to anger I am producing the righteousness of God and living out his will for me. I am loving Ryan. When I am slow to become angry I am ultimately showing my husband covenant love and I am trusting God's Word beyond my own feelings.

4. Put Away All Filthiness and Rampant Wickedness

This phrase tells me to get rid of my short-fused, cold-shoulder-giving, sassy, cutting remarks. It's not always easy for me to respond slowly and edit what I say. Nor is it easy to respond obediently to God's Word rather than from my own feelings. But praise God, he is sanctifying me and showing me how to live.

Instead I am to "*receive* with *meekness* the implanted Word which is able to save your souls" (1:21, emphasis added). When I humbly and gently receive God's Word as my authority and instruction, I am recognizing his sovereignty in my life.

Finally, James tells me to be a doer of the Word and not only a hearer. Doing the Word means honest and loving communication. It's responding from what I heard in my slow-to-anger moment—be patient and kind. Endure the hard conversations and speak intentionally.

With intentionality comes honesty, but fear not, my friends! Being secure in Christ and fiercely devoted to your covenant frees you to be transparent with each other. This is especially true when you know the issue at hand is messy and tough. Because of Jesus, you don't need to avoid hard conversations, and with his help you can speak truth in love (Eph. 4:15). Truth is always the most loving thing you can share, but *how* you say it can sometimes be less than loving. Truth always builds up, but take care not to let the messenger (you, your tone) get in the way. Paul writes:

> Let no corrupting talk come out of your mouths, but only such as is good for building up, as fits the occasion, that it may give grace to those who hear. (Eph. 4:29)

There are times when Ryan puts my whole being at ease through his understanding of Scripture and his understanding of *me*. With patience and kindness, he points me back to Jesus, where I can find all that I need. My affection for Jesus strengthens, and my love for Ryan grows. Thankfully, Ryan will attest that these roles are often reversed in our marriage. He, too, needs help, and by God's grace I'm able to provide it.

The Wisdom in When

Knowing *when* to communicate is vital to facilitating great conversation. Just as we must be intentional in listening and speaking, we also must be able to choose right timing. Certain topics tend to be loaded: finances, sex, in-laws, and daily chores are a few areas that cause tension for us. Maybe you agree? It's taken Ryan and me years of arguments to finally realize that not all timing is created equal. A valuable proverb says,

> A person finds joy in giving an apt reply—
> and how good is a timely word! (Prov. 15:23 NIV)

The ESV translation says it like this: "a word in season, how good it is!" Just as some trees will not bear fruit out of season, certain conversations are unproductive at the wrong time. Having good timing cannot be overemphasized when dealing with sensitive or frustrating topics in marriage. As Ryan mentioned, you have direct access to each other's hearts, and when your timing is off, you're more likely to miss or misread signals and have your communication corrupted by your sinful natures.

We've discovered that good timing helps communication in two ways, each depending on the nature of the conversation to be had. First, it's always a good time to repent and reconnect if you're distant. If and when Ryan and I have a fight—big or small—we try our best to resolve it quickly and efficiently. Over the years we have become faster at fighting. This involves a ton of swallowing anger and pride, but it's always worth the pain. God's instruction to do this is for our own good. Small offenses left unresolved have a tendency to fester. Harboring bitterness and resentment is costly.

The second way good timing helps our communication is by ensuring we both have the space in our hearts, minds, and time to deal with heavier problems. We've found it immensely helpful to make "talk dates" with each other. Ryan has often said to me in the morning, "Can we talk tonight? I have something I need to talk to you about." I'm always happy but slightly nervous to oblige. I'll ask him, "What's it about?" He usually gives me a rough idea—but not always. It depends on the topic. Either way, knowing that he has something on his heart he wants to share helps me prepare my own. We earmark the time (usually within twenty-four hours of one of us bringing something up) and I can approach it with the mental and emotional readiness needed to be fully engaged. This doesn't guarantee an easier conversation, but it does promise to make it healthier. More importantly, knowing ahead of time gives me a chance to pray and ask the Holy Spirit to work in our hearts and guide our talk.

Life is busy, messy, and downright intense at times, so we won't always have the perfect moment for perfectly clear communication. Faithful communication with God is irreplaceable for good communication in marriage. Spending time in Scripture (listening) and in prayer (talking) connects us to God. It gets his Word hidden in our hearts, so when the time comes to talk about the big and small stuff in life, we can do so out of his truth, wisdom (James 1:5), peace (John 14:27), and assurance (Heb. 10:22).

Since you have been raised with Christ (Col. 3:1), fix your focus on God's higher ways. Even when emotions are high and communication proves difficult, you can rest secure in Christ, choose wisdom, and give grace. You are abundantly free to love through how you listen and speak. So keep talking to each other through the hard times! Tough conversations are often diffused by simply being quick to listen and slow to speak with right timing. Keep dialogue going and stay engaged. With Christ you will work through every communication breakdown.

Why Communicate?

In marriage, the goal of communicating is relational intimacy and the goal of talking through conflict is always reconciliation, not retaliation. In the instance of the stinky fish garbage I was plotting retaliation, stewing about the injustice of the situation. I very much want justice and equality in everything, which makes reconciliation less appealing to me. But retaliation is *never* productive. It never brings us closer or moves us forward in our relationship. At best, it stalls us where we are, and at worst, it takes us backward.

Retaliation is always selfish, but reconciliation is a steady marker of covenant love. Reconciliation is intimate. It's not hidden, necessarily, but always private. It is one-on-one. As married people in a communication funk, we can only realign our hearts and restore our friendship by dealing with the issue at hand, repenting, and forgiving. We must talk, listen, and respond in word and action. That communication process is intimate, it's face-to-face, and it's exclusive.

As Jesus instructed, "If your brother sins against you, go and tell him his fault, between you and him alone. If he listens to you, you have gained your brother" (Matt. 18:15). Jesus's language is interesting here. He says to *tell him* (speak clearly), *between you and him alone* (in privacy), and if he *listens* (responds), you have *gained your brother* (you have been reconciled). Jesus is saying that talking and listening are necessary when someone is sinned against. We need to hash it out, and if both parties engage with each other we will reestablish our bond—we will be *reconciled*. It isn't always easy to be reconciled in the moment, and sometimes it's very painful. But despite every communication difficulty, reconciliation is the only loving way forward. Take hope, my friends, for there is a deep joy to be experienced in reconciliation. It's a level of love and affection reserved for you and your spouse to share because of your covenant.

Never Stop Exploring

Selena has covered how to work through communication breakdowns, but there's another—perhaps more common—communication pitfall many couples face: losing curiosity.

Pamela and James had the best kind of start to their relationship. They began as work friends, but over time it blossomed into more as they spoke and listened to each other with genuine curiosity. Their desire to deeply know one another compelled them to study and learn even the smallest details about each other. Their early friendship proved to be a solid foundation for their courtship. Eventually they got married, bought a house, had two kids, and settled in for a long, happy life together—all with their trademark enthusiasm. Over time, however, their curiosity waned. They became complacent with each other and preoccupied with their careers. Their communication suffered as they grew further and further apart until, finally, their friendship was completely cold. It took reaching the brink of divorce for them to realize that their marriage couldn't survive without friendship, and their friendship required intentional, curious communication—the kind that brought them together in the first place. It wasn't easy, but in time they relearned how to be constant studiers of each other, how to stay curious, and how to be genuine friends.

C. S. Lewis wrote in *The Four Loves*, "Friendship is . . . the instrument by which God reveals to each of us the beauties of others."[1] If your friendship is the instrument—the tool—used to be utterly known to each other, your communication determines how often you wield it. Healthy marriages are based on healthy friendships, and healthy friendships always include intentional communication. Selena and I have found the same to be true for us. When our communication falters, our friendship suffers and so does our marriage.

Take a moment and think about when you first met. You likely began as friends, and as your friendship grew, your affection grew. You spent more and more time together exploring the depths of your personalities, interests, desires, and faith. At some point you decided you knew (and enjoyed) enough about each other that you wanted to spend your lives together. It was an exciting pursuit, filled with the desire to deepen your bond of friendship to the point of promising to spend your lives together. What a remarkable thing to recall!

Sadly, many marriages stagnate because couples stop exploring each other. They stop actively investigating, learning, and pursuing. Why is that a common tendency? Familiarity makes us lax, and routines, habits, tiredness, and general lack of creativity or skill are all contributors to poor communication. But you have a lifetime to discover each other, and discoveries are always rife with anticipation and excitement. You need only persist down your path of friendship!

If a couple spends two years dating and fifty years married, it stands to reason that they have much more to discover about each other within marriage than not. That's the wonder of communication: it is a skill and a tool useful for exploring another person's heart. And, of course, within marriage there are no bounds to what you can find; there's no limit to where your friendship can go.

Friendship is rewarding, but here's the bottom line: intentional communication takes work. Both of you must be engaged and willing to speak honestly, with energy and eagerness to discover what's around the next bend. The best way to find out new information is easy: just ask.

We're big fans of unusual and probing conversation starters. Questions like, "Who would you most (or least) enjoy being stuck in an elevator with?" and "If time froze for everyone but you for one day, what would you do?" offer interesting ways to gain new glimpses into your spouse's personality, interests, and passions. We also like to ask the same simple series of questions at the dinner table each night (we ask our kids as well; their answers are always illuminating and often hilarious): What was the best part of your day? What was the worst? Why? Conversation starters like these are simple tools that help spur intentional communication.

Intentionality also has to do with setting the stage (appropriate timing and atmosphere) for whatever you're hoping to discuss. But it doesn't happen automatically. You must purpose to break and make habits and routines in the name of friendship.

Of course, nothing is more valuable than knowing what God is doing in each other's heart. Ask each other questions aimed at rooting out where you both are spiritually. What have you been learning in God's Word? How does it help you understand the gospel more clearly? Has the Holy Spirit been convicting you of sin or disbelief? In what areas, and why? How is your personal prayer life?

Asking intentional questions is the quickest way toward purposeful conversation. Remember, you don't want your spouse to feel like they're being interrogated, so be wise with your timing and tone.

Finally, rest, have fun, and laugh together. Laughter is a common component of every friendship. It sprouts happiness and lightens the heart. Don't take yourselves too seriously. Remember, God is in control. Jesus secured your identity and salvation on the cross. Every breath is an extraordinary gift from the God of the universe. He is sovereign, so you don't have to be. There is nothing you can't talk through with Christ as the center of your marriage. Rest easy in his endless supply of grace and love. Weep as often as you need, encourage and explore each other, laugh as much as you can, and enjoy God's gracious gift of communication in your marriage.

FOR REFLECTION

- What signals do you miss with your spouse? Ask yourself, then ask each other.
- How can you communicate more intentionally with your spouse?
- How can the gospel affect the way you deal with communication breakdowns?
- What's one area in which you hit it out of the park in terms of communication?

7

Money and Stewardship

Gaining Agreement and Creating Vision
for Your Finances

> I have held many things in my hands, and I have
> lost them all; but whatever I have placed in God's
> hands, that I still possess.
>
> Martin Luther

It was a cool night on our apartment patio when God and
I had our reckoning. Selena and I had just moved to sunny
Southern California to start a business, and the process had
left us strapped for cash. We had nothing—or so I felt. In
fact, we had less than nothing; debt and bills piled high and
our income was far less than we needed to cover them. That's
why I sat outside complaining to God. No exaggeration: we
had twenty-three dollars in our bank account, rent was due

the next day, and our car payment was due shortly after. I was afraid and mad at God.

Not only were we financially exhausted but our emotions were in tatters. We were both college-educated, we worked hard, and we had left good jobs back home—for what? For this? The American Dream felt like a nightmare. I felt demoralized and emasculated because I couldn't provide for my bride. We argued about money and our lack. I'd often spend long hours working through the night to make deadlines in hopes that my clients would pay me in time to cover next month's bills. Our communication suffered as I buried myself in my work. Selena found respite at a local riding facility where she could have community and enjoy some equestrian therapy. Things were not good in our marriage.

That evening I sat outside (as I often do) deep in thought, watching the trees sway in the breeze. My stomach was in knots as I anxiously considered ways to make ends meet. This wasn't the first time we'd been on the brink of financial ruin, nor would it be our last. But it was, by God's grace, the last time I worried hopelessly about our finances.

God is forever faithful. He speaks to us in ways we will hear him best. I didn't hear God's audible voice, but it was clearer than if he were sitting right next to me. Like a father speaking to a toddler, God got down on my level and injected my heart with peace in a way I could finally understand: *You are not your provider, I am.* My stress began to lift. *It doesn't matter how hard you work, how skilled or clever you are, or how much you stress about money—you are not your own provider. I am.*

Suddenly the gorilla on my back disappeared. I felt light and free, utterly resigned to trusting God. My fists unclenched and the blood drained from my hands. My anxiety turned to joy, my fear to faith. I finally began to understand what it means to trust in Jehovah-Jireh—"the LORD will provide."

Did we get a letter from the credit card company erasing our debt? Nope! Did God provide in his perfect timing so we could diligently and wisely pay back what we owed? Absolutely. Did we learn how to trust him and have peace in the storm? In ways we never imagined. That night God began the process of prying my fingers off our money. Even today, when I begin to put too much of my security in our bank balance and my grip begins to tighten, God always lovingly—sometimes painfully—reminds me that I am not our provider, he is.

That was one of the most pivotal moments in my life as a husband, and because of that, in our marriage. It marks the start of our journey of learning about biblical stewardship and understanding what it means to truly believe that God is who he says he is: King of all, our Provider, and our Giver of Peace.

Is Enough Ever Enough?

Money is consistently cited as a leading cause of stress in marriage and discord between spouses. If you haven't felt it yet, you probably will. If you have felt it, it's important to understand the root sources of financial stress and equip yourselves with tools to deal with them.

One would think that financial stress would closely correlate to particular life phases. We expect to be a little more strapped for cash when we're young and poor, but we also expect life to get easier later on, when we're more established and earning a higher income. However, the data proves otherwise. In 2010, the American Psychological Association (APA) performed a study on stress that revealed 76 percent of people across all generations are anxious about money. Financial stress seems perpetual, regardless of how established you are. "Enough" money is never enough to buy peace, or at least that's what the study suggests.

The APA discovery runs contrary to everything modern consumerism teaches us to believe: "If you work hard, earn enough, buy the right things, and put money away, you will be happy." This is anecdotally true as well. How many times have you heard stories of unhappy wealthy people? As the saying goes, "You can't buy happiness," or in slightly more modern phrasing, "Mo' money, mo' problems."

It's easy to read those words and heartily agree. But do we live it *functionally*? I would argue that if you're perpetually stressed about finances—if it's an ongoing source of marital strife—you're buying the lie that money satisfies on some level. That's not meant to make you feel guilty; God knows it's a constant struggle in our household! We can all find room for growth and deeper trust in God when it comes to money.

Financial Stressors in Marriage

The reasons for nonstop financial stress are numerous. Spending habits, life choices, fear, and external factors like the job market, inflation, or life hardships can all play a role. We often overestimate how much control we have over our financial well-being. Even a "secure" job can be suddenly lost for unforeseen reasons. One tragic accident or sickness can drain your entire savings account overnight and send you reeling into medical debt and financial chaos.

If we find our identity and security in our bank balance, we risk losing both.

One common reason married couples experience perpetual financial stress is unchecked consumerism and comparison. This leads to "lifestyle inflation." The concept is simple: when we have more, we spend more—we *want* more. Instead of reaching a certain lifestyle and being content, we tend to look to the next best thing: a nicer house, a newer car, a fancier set of appliances—you name it.

If we are consumers, we purchase new products because of their perceived benefits (whether the benefits are true or not). If we're comparers, we buy things to keep up with trends, friends, or societal expectations. There is always something newer, nicer, or fancier to buy; that is never going to change. What can change, however, is the human heart.

We can't control what happens to us or culture's pressure toward consumerism. We can only employ wise money management principles and choose to put our identity, worth, and security in Christ alone. The former will affect our financial decision making and the latter our peace and joy.

The One Perspective That Changes Everything

As a married couple, your chief aim should be to align your view of money with God's, and to be completely unified in doing so. God has an opinion about your finances. He also wants your eternal best. The more you place your trust in him, the greater your freedom and the more your marriage will flourish.

So, what is God's view of money? What is its purpose in your life? In the world? And finally, how can you and your spouse find agreement in such a contentious area? As I mentioned above, God lovingly began to help me understand biblical stewardship that night on our patio.

Biblical stewardship is the idea that God owns everything, and what we do "possess" in this life is that which is temporarily entrusted into our care. What we have is never truly ours to own—we are called to be *stewards*. As the psalmist writes, "The earth is the LORD's and the fullness thereof, the world and those who dwell therein" (Ps. 24:1). Even in one of the first commands given to Adam and Eve in the garden they were instructed to "subdue" the earth—to care for the creation in which God placed them. They were granted authority but not ownership.

When we relinquish ownership and embrace our roles as commissioned stewards, our grip loosens from around our finances and freedom overwhelms our souls. For the steward, everything in life is a gift of inexhaustible grace. Secure in God's abundance, we are freed to live openhanded lives and place our full trust in his sovereignty. God can give and God can take away, but the steward's posture of worship never changes.

When we were struggling to scrape by and I started embracing my role as a steward, my attitude toward work shifted. Instead of anxiously striving I worked with joy, knowing that God was ultimately in control of providing more clients and projects. Whatever work I did have to do (what little it was), I saw as an opportunity to honor God—to work hard for his glory instead of mine.

He promised he would provide for our every need according to his plan and purposes (Phil. 4:19). Did I *actually* believe him? When we worry deeply in our hearts—as evidenced through constant financial stress—we're disbelieving God's promise.

I find it comforting that Jesus's disciples worried too. But it's even more comforting to know that his loving correction of them also applies to us today:

> And do not seek what you are to eat and what you are to drink, nor be worried. For all the nations of the world seek after these things, and your Father knows that you need them. Instead, seek his kingdom, and these things will be added to you. (Luke 12:29–31)

Jesus knew money would be a constant struggle in the hearts of believers. Of his thirty-eight parables, sixteen are about possessions and money. In the four gospels, 288 verses directly deal with the topic. In the whole of the Bible, five hundred verses address prayer, fewer than five hundred verses talk about faith, and more than two thousand verses are on money or possessions. When Scripture places such a strong emphasis on any one topic, we'd better perk up our ears and listen!

Do You *Love* Money?

One of the most often quoted passages about money is 1 Timothy 6:10: "For the love of money is a root of all kinds of evils. It is through this craving that some have wandered away from the faith and pierced themselves with many pangs." Money is not intrinsically evil; *loving* it is. It is evil to become emotionally entangled with it, to trust it, and to overvalue it. Augustine of Hippo called all sin "disordered love." Loving money—or anything—more than Jesus is sin, and will create chaos in your marriage.

It's not always easy to know or admit when we "love" money; most people don't consciously place their identity or security in it. Few are blatantly greedy or money-grubbing. The real-life love of money is usually subtle and oftentimes harmless to your day-to-day existence. That's precisely why God can use your marriage and the financial stress between you and your spouse to diagnose—and treat—sickness in your heart as he lovingly reminds you of his sovereignty.

Take a moment and ask yourself these questions:

- What causes the most tension in your marriage? Is it somehow connected to your income?
- Are arguments rooted in differing ideas of how to manage money, like saving, giving, or spending?
- Do either of you experience fear of lack or missing out on the next big thing?
- How about functional greed or a never-ending desire for more?
- Are you consciously content, or is that a foreign concept?
- Does comparing to others cause you to spend compulsively?

Whatever your source of financial stress, the root cause is always an underlying disbelief or dissatisfaction in Jesus.

That is why every financial fight is an opportunity to remind each other of the gospel—that Christ is enough and God will provide every good thing you need. The gospel must be your baseline—your common pursuit. Instead of reacting negatively and escalating whatever financial issue you're dealing with, you can remind yourself and your spouse of God's promises and your greater purpose in his kingdom. Doing so dethrones money and releases its stronghold. It diminishes as Christ increases. Jesus again becomes the chief goal, cause, and pursuit in your lives, while money is simply a tool to be used for his glory.

Selena's Discovery

SELENA

When Ryan and I got married, he knew how much I loved horses. He's grown much more savvy about the equestrian disciplines I love most. He even has his favorite Olympic showjumping horse and rider combination. As a kid, I remember the first time I saw an equestrian competition on TV. I just *knew* I had to ride and jump big beautiful horses. From then on, I asked for riding lessons, riding clothes, and time at the barn. I did anything I could to ride; I cleaned tack, cleaned stalls, groomed horses—whatever would get me on the back of a horse. Riding became a big part of my life and eventually my identity.

In the first five years of our marriage Ryan agreed to let me purchase my first horse: *my first horse*. It was a dream come true. I was always proud to talk about my horse, about our training, lessons, shows, and so on. Once I got my first "real" job where I made "real" money, all my horse dreams began coming true. But it was at the expense of my marriage, my relationship with God, and my identity. Losing myself in the world of horses provided me with only temporary happiness and contentment.

139

Before we moved out of Washington, Ryan was spending more than twenty hours a week volunteering at church, so I would go to the barn after work. At the time it seemed normal to be away from each other so much. We were only a few years into it and naïvely thought we were doing everything God wanted. But we couldn't help wonder why this path we were on felt so alone, burdensome, and empty.

Before moving to Southern California, we sold my horse, rented out our house, and took a minimalistic approach to life—we could fit only a small amount into the back of our tiny U-Haul trailer. It was more expensive to ride in California, so I did the next best thing and photographed riders and horses. I became a professional equestrian photographer for magazines and traveled around the country to get "the story" or to have my name next to those photos or on the cover of that magazine—the cost didn't matter. All that mattered was that I purchased whatever I needed when I needed it. New and *now* is how I wanted it, and the price tag was a menial distraction. My identity depended on my being at the next major equestrian event. I felt like less of a person if I turned down a job. I would stress if I wasn't overloaded with clients to shoot for. Needless to say, I became a slave to this idol because if it failed, I would be a failure. Or so I thought.

All of this put tension on our marriage. I'd constantly argue with Ryan about why I needed to buy this lens or go to that event. We spent weeks apart. He was the brake pedal and I was a lead-footed gas masher. My identity was rooted in horses, competition, and expensive photography gear—all good things gone bad. They dethroned God in my heart. My marriage was suffering, our finances looked bleak, and

I constantly felt the heaviness of it all. I wasn't swimming; I was simply trying not to drown.

But God is good, faithful, ridiculously patient, and unconditionally loving. After we had our first daughter, Dela, my heart was pulled in two different directions. A big horse show was just around the corner and my baby was three months old. I struggled to balance mom life and my job. I had assignments lined up. *I can do this*, I thought. Dela had other plans. I quickly discovered something had to give—and it wouldn't be my baby girl.

Stepping away from photography was slow and painful, but absolutely necessary. After about a year of my walking away, turning down assignments, and giving jobs to other photographer friends, God transformed and renewed my heart. He showed me just how much he is our provider and the only one we should find our identity in. His unfailing love changed my heart and perspective toward our finances. It was right about then that Proverbs 31 took on a whole new meaning for me. Its verses painted a picture of the wife I wanted to be and could be because of who Jesus is. More specifically, I saw the verses about how she worked in her home and how she dealt with finances. She handled them in a way that flowed from security and strength, not fear or lack. My heart longed to be that wife, the one my husband trusts, the one who considers a field and buys it (v. 16), the one who opens her hand to the poor (v. 20). The one who does not fear snow because her household is clothed in scarlet (v. 21). This is the wife I knew God intended me to be.

However, becoming a godly wife in the area of finance meant relinquishing control and understanding that I am a steward of this life, and more specifically, my marriage. It took me years to understand and rest securely in the fact that I already had everything I needed in the person and work of Jesus Christ. As God grew my faith, my confidence and security now came from him and not the bottom line of our checkbook or the next event I was supposed to photograph. The more God entrusted to us, the more I wanted to steward it well. I wanted Ryan to trust me to not do him harm in this area. He's not just the bill payer, he's my husband, and I want his heart to rest in the fact that I'm also using wisdom and discernment.

Our money is not a tool to prove how great we are or how well we're doing financially. And it's not a way to get meaning in life as I once thought. Everything in our care belongs to God; we are called to act as glad stewards. This single heart change has exponentially increased our joy, relaxed our anxiety, and unified our efforts as a married couple.

Will we own a horse again? Maybe one day. Do I still do photography? Absolutely, but mostly for fun and for close friends and family. This is how I steward these areas well in our current state of life and I could not be more grateful.

First Why, Then How

RYAN

For Selena and me, nothing has brought greater clarity to how we manage our money than biblical stewardship. We've briefly covered its principles, so how should you apply them? It's tempting to be too prescriptive, and I want to avoid that. What works for one couple may not work for another. There are countless ways to apply gospel priorities, godly wisdom, and biblical stewardship to your finances. How you do it is ultimately between you, your spouse, and God.

With that said, I want to be transparent and share what has worked for us. At the very least, I hope our example provides a sense of stewardship in real life. At the most, you may find an idea or two to help you in your own journey as faithful stewards.

At this point you may feel compelled to create a budget if you haven't done so already. While budgets are good, they only outline *how* you will spend your money. Knowing how will accomplish little to battle financial stress unless you're clear and in agreement about *why*. Before you create a budget, you need a vision.

The first step in creating a financial vision is to have a candid conversation. You may not realize how different your views of money are. One of you may be a natural saver and the other a natural spender. If one of you grew up in relative poverty and the other with plenty, you will disagree on what is "necessary" and what isn't. Discuss your upbringing, how your parents handled money, and how it may have shaped your views today.

Pray together for sensitivity toward the Holy Spirit and God's Word, then dive into Scripture. Find out what God says about provision. Here's a start:

- God will supply your every need (Phil. 4:19).
- Don't be anxious; trust God to know your need and provide for it best (Matt. 6:31–32).
- God withholds no good thing. Rest in his timing and trust his ways (Ps. 84:11).
- Ask as a child. God is a good, generous Father (Matt. 7:11; John 16:24).

143

Lock these verses (and others like them) away in your hearts and allow the authority of Scripture to bear weight in your life—*internalize* it. Take time to list passages that remind you of God's promises to provide. These will be touchstones for future reference—your timely reminders—when you feel financial stress creeping in. Next, list passages about handling abundance. How are you called to be generous? This list will provide the absolute standard for the purposes of money and practices of wise stewardship.

Finally, write down principles *in your own words* that will guide your financial activity. They may prove difficult to articulate at first, but just start writing. Pray and listen for the Holy Spirit to prompt you. If it helps, you can start each statement with "As stewards, we are called to . . ."

Include statements that speak to your current situation. If you often argue about money, articulate how you're called to peace. If you tend to make unwise purchases or overspend, include wisdom and self-control in your principles. Be honest with yourselves, and refer back to your two lists of passages for guidance.

When Is Enough, Enough? Our Two-Budget Approach

With your vision in hand, you can now create a budget. For many, this is an obvious practice, and you've already done the work. For Selena and me, not so much. We didn't figure out an effective budgeting method until over a decade into our marriage. We've since devised a modified system that works for us. I encourage you use the same discretion. Avoid getting bogged down trying to adopt a tool that won't work. The goal is to find a way forward, even if it's a little unconventional. Ours is done with good old-fashioned pen and paper. (Check out our website for budgeting resources and good books on family finance.)

We've created two separate budgets: one for our current financial situation and another for our "ideal" scenario sometime in the future. We call them our "functional budget" and our "future budget."

The Functional Budget

Our functional budget includes categories of monthly expenses: rent/mortgage, food, transportation (car payment, auto insurance, fuel), utilities, insurance, fun, and so on. We know with pretty good accuracy how much we should be spending in each area so we don't overextend ourselves. We've also included margin for unforeseen expenses like replacing a windshield or an urgent home repair. Even though we don't keep a close eye on every penny, we know pretty quickly if we're approaching our limit in any of the categories. If you don't have a functional budget, I definitely recommend you create one and use it as a tool for wise money management in your marriage.

The problem with functional (traditional) budgets is that they can contribute to the "lifestyle inflation" described earlier. As your income increases, your margin—the extra—will do the same. If you're like us, you have lots of nonessential desires that can soak up those additional funds if you let them. If you fail to remind yourselves of your purpose and identity in light of the gospel, you can fall into consumerism or comparison, which will lead to unwise decision making and bad stewardship. For example, an extra three hundred dollars each month could suddenly represent the payment on that car you've been looking at—even if there is nothing wrong with the car(s) you already own! If you're not careful, this cycle will repeat without end. Every pay bump or expense decrease is quickly swallowed up by more spending.

I'm not saying that upgrading your car (or home, or anything else) is intrinsically wrong, only that the decision to do so should be deliberate and strategic—made on purpose, *for a purpose*, and always in light of gospel priorities. This is where your "future budget" is vital. It serves one simple function in your life: to define *enough*.

The Future Budget

Our future budget is part of our family vision, which describes our mission and calling to reach people with the message of the gospel. The critical question we asked was, "What is the optimal budget for the area we're called to and the people we're called to reach?" This helped us identify an eventual cap for our life expenses and curb unwise lifestyle inflation. It helps us clearly answer the question, "How much is enough?"

Our future budget changes as God sanctifies us (aligns our hearts more with Christ's) and our calling becomes clearer. As a habit, we review and revise it before every major life change and at the end of each year. Doing so helps us to be as generous as possible while also exercising wisdom in saving for future events.

If ever we reach our future budget, we are freed to give everything else away instead of amassing a pile of cash by default. Saving, while good, can become an idol if we're not careful, especially if fear is our underlying motivation. What if giving, instead of saving, became your primary financial goal? What if you could give half or even 90 percent of your income away? A future budget can help you identify if or when that might be possible and appropriate.

Getting Even More Practical—Stewarding as One

It's one thing to establish a vision; it's another to implement it. Your vision and budgets began with a candid conversation and should continue the same way.

When Selena and I were first married, we had no vision. We had no budget. We had no clue about biblical stewardship or how to actively seek agreement in our finances. Our spending was sporadic and often unguided. Paying bills felt like a fire drill. We lived hand-to-mouth and thought it was normal. This was partly because we were both full-time students working low-paying jobs, but it was also due to our youthful ignorance.

Thankfully, God used our naïveté to teach us many valuable lessons. I often wish we could have learned them an easier way! Thus, here are a few practical things we've learned in our journey toward stewarding "as one."

Sacrificial, Cheerful Giving

One mark of the faithful steward is a radically generous heart. Consider the apostle Paul's words to believers in Corinth:

The point is this: whoever sows sparingly will also reap sparingly, and whoever sows bountifully will also reap bountifully. Each one must give as he has decided in his heart, not reluctantly or under compulsion, for God loves a cheerful giver. And God is able to make all grace abound to you, so that having all sufficiency in all things at all times, you may abound in every good work. (2 Cor. 9:6–8)

Notice the emphasis Paul places on the attitude of the heart. He doesn't prescribe an amount or percentage. How much we give is not important to God. He cares about our hearts. We are called to give sacrificially (you should *feel* its impact in your own life) in response to the gospel for the perpetuation of the gospel.

As a couple, discuss how you are called to give. It might be a set amount each month, a percentage of your income, or a mix of the two. Whatever you decide in your hearts to give should be given faithfully, sacrificially, and cheerfully.

Paul continues with an apt reminder to believers:

He who supplies seed to the sower and bread for food will supply and multiply your seed for sowing and increase the harvest of your righteousness. You will be enriched in every way to be generous in every way, which through us will produce thanksgiving to God. (vv. 10–11)

Giving sacrificially builds reliance on God and *multiplies the harvest of your righteousness*. It doesn't multiply your righteousness itself but rather its *harvest*—the fruit of your life as a new creation and someone already adopted into God's eternal family.

Take time to pray together. Decide in your hearts how you will give. Challenge each other to be generous, sacrificial, and cheerful. Seek agreement in this area. If you or your spouse find it impossible to give in such a way, turn to Jesus and ask God to transform your hearts.

Should We Share Accounts?

The Bible doesn't explicitly tell couples to share bank accounts, and most secular financial experts will advise you to keep them separate. Is there a "right" way? Not definitively—but I do think there is a wise way. Joining accounts can be a beautiful representation of your trust, unity, and commitment as husband and wife. It's not a primary issue in the Christian life, but I do believe it's an important one for your marriage.

When you and your spouse become "one flesh," everything changes. You are utterly and completely merged. Your individuality remains to an extent, but your existence is no longer exclusive to yourselves; it's inclusive of one another. There is a beautiful mingling of hearts, souls, and bodies that only happens in marriage. How much more should your finances be comingled?

Despite our many mistakes, merging accounts was one of the first things we did after our honeymoon. I'm so glad we did. Our paychecks (and our expenses) were no longer ours individually but ours as a couple. From that moment on we earned, saved, gave, and spent as a single unit—as a family.

Many couples have written to us asking for the "right approach." As I mentioned, Scripture doesn't give a definitive answer. However, I do believe wisdom and the desire for unity make the decision clear. Here's why: keeping separate accounts can divide more than your finances. "My money" and "your money" can create an imbalance of financial control that may lead to unhealthy leverage over the spouse who earns less. Separate bank statements can lead to secrecy in spending. Finally, splitting bills (such as rent and utilities) is against the spirit of selflessness and unity in marriage (not to mention the logistical headaches it can cause).

It's up to you to decide whether or not you will share accounts in your marriage. We recommend you do.

Creating Conversation Thresholds (Making Hard Talks Easier)

One way to balance freedom and trust is to establish spending thresholds as conversation triggers. For instance, Selena and I have a pre-established amount that neither of us will spend without talking about it first. It's high enough to grant individual freedom and discretion but low enough to allow active conversation about spending beyond our normal budget.

This principle applies to our giving as well. Many times, one of us will feel a particular burden to help a friend, family member, cause, or organization. Discussing our discretionary giving (that which is beyond our tithe) allows us to share in the joy and glad burden of loving our neighbors as Christ has loved us. It also provides us the opportunity to agree in prayer with joined hearts as a family contending for those who need help.

Handling Expenses and Bills

Another important conversation to have is when bills will be paid and which of you will make it happen. Early on in our marriage, Selena made sure our bills were paid on time. After we had kids I took over the responsibility because it made more sense for us. This may seem like an obvious recommendation, but there were many times when our bills were paid late and our credit suffered simply because we each assumed the other took care of it. Work out a system that works for you, then stick to it. If ever an unexpected expense appears that raises concern, discuss it and tackle the problem head-on, together.

Freedom to Enjoy

Discussing money and stewardship can cause us to feel guilty for material comforts we have in this life. We must reject guilt and replace it with gratitude. It is good and right to enjoy God's gifts with grateful hearts, because he alone gives them. If a parent gives a gift to his child, he is most honored when that gift is received and enjoyed. In the same way, we are not to reject or feel ashamed for God's gifts. Instead, we are free to receive. He delights in our delight.

The key to wise and joy-filled stewardship in your marriage is *context*. All the right choices, plans, and budgets will provide little peace if done outside your greatest calling as followers of Christ: to enjoy God and amplify his glory. Whatever you possess in this life—or rather, whatever has been entrusted to your care—is to be enjoyed as a good and gracious gift from a loving, generous God. When you partake in God's provision in light of his goodness, your joy becomes limitless and your thanksgiving bountiful.

> For everything created by God is good, and nothing is to be rejected if it is received with thanksgiving, for it is made holy by the word of God and prayer. (1 Tim. 4:4–5)

Everything you have is a gift from God. Everything. When Jesus is our portion, times of material abundance and times of material lack will always produce gratitude in our hearts. We are tasked as stewards to use what we have—however much or little—for his glory, and that includes enjoying what he has given us! There is no formula, only Jesus and the counsel of the Holy Spirit. In all things, seek agreement with each other. Live wisely, steward diligently, and rest in God's gracious provision in Christ. As you do, the particulars will become less important, and the peace of God will reign over every area of your marriage—even your finances.

FOR REFLECTION

- Do you often stress about your income or expenses? Why?
- How does the idea of stewardship help or challenge you in the way you view finances in your marriage?
- Are there areas within your finances where stewardship could take precedence? How would stewardship specifically affect that area?

8

Intimacy and Sex

Experiencing Each Other to the Glory of God

> Within the context of covenant love and mutual
> service, no amount of passion is excessive.
>
> Betsy Ricucci

When I was a young man, my dad gave me two ultimatums:
no tattoos and no sex before marriage. As it turned out,
his first ultimatum wasn't very ultimate—my dad, brother,
and I got matching tats together—but the second one stuck.
He used *very* colorful language when warning me about
sex before marriage. I vaguely remember something about
a dull, rusty machete and me joining a monastery. I knew he
was exaggerating (*I hoped*), but he got through to my thick,
testosterone-soaked teenage brain. You may call him crazy,
but it worked.

I now realize that my dad knew what he was talking about. His perspective was unique. As a counselor, he's worked tirelessly with countless husbands, wives, and children to salvage their lives—*themselves*—from the wreckage of misused and misunderstood sexuality. He knows that culture is at fierce odds with God's model for marriage, sex, and family, and where he watched culture lead, there was often destruction. My dad drew clear boundaries around sex, not out of prudish, arbitrary moralism or to steal my joy but rather because he loved me and wanted to ensure my maximal enjoyment. His kind, albeit overly graphic, warning about sex was rooted in love.

The Power of Sex

Scott and Jennifer went to different colleges, dated plenty, and slept with numerous partners. It wasn't until their midtwenties that they heard the gospel and put their faith in Jesus. They eventually met at a church gathering, struck up a relationship, and the rest is history. Though they abstained from sex with one another until their wedding night, they each carried their sexual histories with them into marriage. They both understood and rested in God's grace over their previous sin, and spiritually they had been made completely new creations (2 Cor. 5:17). However, the emotional and relational consequences of their sexual choices were still a factor in their marriage. Jennifer struggled with intimacy because of negative sexual experiences with a past boyfriend. Scott's previous sexual encounters and a past pornography addiction skewed his expectations of what Jennifer should do in bed. Their sex life was marked by frustration and pain. Instead of unifying them, their intimacy drove them further apart. By God's grace they found healing through godly counseling, church community, and prayer, but it took years of hard work.

Would Scott and Jennifer have had a perfect sex life if they had never had sex before marriage? Probably not. However, they'd be the first to tell you that their previous sexual experiences weren't worth it. The short-term pleasure and "freedom" of sex before marriage came at a far greater cost than either of them imagined. They're now closer than ever, and they're thankful for God's grace in hindsight. However, if given the opportunity, they'd gladly have saved sex for their marriage covenant.

Sex is as good as it is powerful. I've come to view sexuality like a sort of atomic force: in its proper place, it binds you together, but when wielded without caution it levels cities and the fallout renders them uninhabitable. We must be careful to understand God's design for sex and its role in marriage while grasping our cultural context. Sex is a gift and a blessing, but just as with any gift, it must be stewarded with wisdom. When we understand God's parameters around and purpose for sexuality, our enjoyment is maximized and God's glory amplified.

Sex and intimacy are unlike any other aspect of your marriage. They are exclusively yours, neither one to be shared nor breached. Sex is the one activity explicitly and exclusively reserved for you and your spouse. It is the physical manifestation of your intimacy on every level. It literally unites your bodies and is a representation of your trust, vulnerability, passion, and generosity toward each other. Sex within marriage is sex as God intended—an expression and reinforcement of your exclusive covenant, purposed for your pleasure and the perpetuation of generations. The institution that contains sex—marriage—is the same one where children are raised, discipled, and equipped to flourish. Finally, sex is a glimpse of the intimacy and unity—the *wonder* and *joy* of relationship—experienced in the Trinity and our eventual union with Christ as his Bride. Indeed, sex is good as God designed!

On the flip side, sex wreaks havoc when mishandled or distorted. Some have diminished the scope of the sexual experience to a primarily physical exchange. Pornography is lauded as harmless by its proponents, who argue that no one gets hurt, but research proving the opposite continues to mount. Porn is now widely accepted by researchers as harmful; it's psychologically, culturally, and physically damaging to everyone involved. The rise of the porn industry has led to exploitation of the weak, the enslavement of the addicted, and a staggering distortion of human sexuality. Oftentimes, the most affected are our children and teens who are trying to find themselves amid the barrage of sexual messaging. Our schools give talks to students about avoiding disease and using contraception. They're taught to practice *safe sex* while its emotional impacts are overlooked.

If we're not watchful, we risk missing the power and potential of sexuality as God designed it. We risk forgoing its full goodness and purpose in exchange for a cheap counterfeit. We risk detaching sex from its greatest joy and deepest purpose whenever we reduce it to a purely physical act. Such reductions are shortsighted and must be rejected. While it is undeniably physical, sex is utterly entangled with every aspect of your being. Your heart, soul, and mind are as much a part of the sexual experience as your body—if not more. Further, your sexual behavior doesn't only affect you; it affects your spouse and your children in profound ways.

A Note on Grace

You may be feeling the effects of distorted sexuality in your marriage, even if it's in your distant past. If that's the case, fear, shame, or dread are likely common guests in your marriage bed. Previous sexual encounters, abuse, addiction, or other perversions of God's design for sex will inevitably affect your physical intimacy as a married couple, but there's hope.

There's always hope.

In Christ, you're not defined by your past; you're defined by his perfect life, death, and resurrection. Whatever your history, God is gracious to heal and restore—to extravagantly redeem—sex in your marriage. He wants to define true intimacy in your marriage for your enjoyment and his glory. Sex is a good gift from an exceedingly great God, and when you experience it in his designed context your pleasure will multiply on every level. Read on knowing you are covered in unending grace.

Three Modern Views of Sexuality

Before discussing practical ideas, it's helpful to understand how culture perceives sexuality. Doing so helps us recognize our own misconceptions and align our hearts with God's worthy design for sex in marriage. Modern views of sex and personal sexuality are really not modern at all; they're ancient. Timothy Keller wrote an excellent paper called "The

Gospel and Sex" that addresses biblical sexuality by contrasting it with three old paradigms he calls sexual realism, sexual platonism, and sexual romanticism. Remnants of each view exist today, and you may have adopted pieces of each into your own perspective of sex. As we will see, all fall short of the full beauty and purpose of God's design, and only the Christian view of sex offers the greatest potential for long-lasting purpose, joy, and fulfillment.

Sexual Realism

Sexual realism dates back to Greco-Roman civilization and emphasizes the physicality of sex. To the realist, sexual desire is a natural physical appetite akin to eating or sleeping, and it should be treated as such. "If it feels right, do it" is an apt motto for the sexual realist. Sex is neither good nor bad, it just is. In his paper, Keller references sex education in public schools as an example of sexual realism. Kids are instructed to embrace and explore their sexuality—whatever it may be—just so long as they do so safely. The term "safe sex" originated in response to the HIV/AIDS epidemic of the 1980s. The safe sex movement started with the sole purpose of preventing the spread of disease and has since evolved to include any practice aimed at preventing infection or unwanted pregnancy. A sexual realist's view emphasizes the physical desire and resulting outcomes of sex but largely ignores its mental, emotional, and spiritual implications.

Sexual Platonism

According to Keller, sexual platonism is at the opposite end of the spectrum and stems from Hellenistic philosophy.

While platonists view sex as carnal, like realists, it's the platonist view that gives *carnal* its negative connotations. Sex is seen as a crude physical indulgence that detracts from more virtuous pursuits of knowledge, awareness, and spirituality.

Here's an awkward illustration: my grandma was a sprightly lady, beautiful to her core, and I loved her very much. She often chased my brother and me around her house with a fly swatter because we fought so much. My grandpa passed away when we were very young, so most of our childhood memories with our grandma were while she dated other men. To this day, my brother and I still laugh as we quote her response whenever we asked about her significant others: "It's platonic!" she would shout with indignation. It was *always* platonic. It wasn't until years later that I learned what she meant. She meant they didn't have sex. (This is *so* weird to write, by the way.)

Given my grandma's generation, her response makes perfect sense. Both her indignation and her insistence were sharp indications of how she, along with many church people, viewed or still view sex. For some (Christians included), sex is an inherently sinful—or shameful—endeavor, regardless of context. This mindset is a form of sexual platonism and it likely contributed to the sexual revolution of the 1960s and '70s, which is characterized by women and men rebelling against perceived sexual repression or traditionally defined sexuality (monogamous heterosexuality, nuclear families). Many Christians struggle with desiring and enjoying sex because they see it as generally bad, which is an unfortunate byproduct of how some church traditions (perhaps unintentionally) adopted and fostered sexual platonism.

Sexual Romanticism

Finally, Keller notes that sexual romanticism is the idea that the desire for sex, like all primal instincts, is inherently good and should be indulged—societal restrictions have only stifled maximum human enjoyment and should be rejected. This view is similar to sexual realism except it promises additional personal meaning by finding and experiencing *pure*, primal urges. Sexual romanticism sees sex as a means for self-actualization and a source of personal fulfillment—a way to be happy in life. Today, this paradigm is evident through oversexualization of popular music, entertainment, and media. Sitcoms and songs idealize men and women who are most in tune with their sexual identities and who act upon their cravings with boldness and candor (inside *or* outside marriage). One's sexuality is tightly intertwined with one's identity, political ideals, and social affiliations—even more so than faith, family, or religion. Sexuality is no longer defined as something you *do* but as a hardwired part of one's biological makeup, and therefore it is a fundamental aspect of who one is as a person. Finally, to the sexual romantic, if something is considered natural it is ultimate, good, and to be pursued at any cost.

Each of the above approaches has hints of truth, but none align sufficiently with the biblical perspective of sexuality. None will produce deep, lasting joy as God intended. If we're to have healthy married sex lives, we must answer a few questions. What is God's view of sexuality? Why should we mold our view of sexuality according to God's? The quick answer is for our good and for God's glory.

As you may have guessed, we're about to explore the longer version of that answer. To start, extraordinarily fulfilling sex and intimacy in marriage begin with this one simple premise:

God designed sex with his purposes, our enjoyment, and his glory in mind.

God's View of Intimacy and Sex

Sex is good. Intimacy is good. God designed both on purpose. As Christians, we aim to glorify God and mirror Christ in every aspect of life, sex included. Every aspect of sex in marriage should aim to accomplish God's purposes by being aligned to his design. We do that by acknowledging and amplifying the purposes for which sex was created, in the place where it's appropriate, and with purity that honors God and each other. As we do, we experience and enjoy the passion of sex on the deepest levels possible.

I could provide platitudes and practical tools to enliven your sex life as a married couple, like "have sex every so often" or "do this and that to have better sex." I could even share candidly about what's helped us. The problem with that approach is it probably wouldn't help you, at least not for long. Every marriage is unique, and blanket to-dos would likely produce anxiety and hinder growth. Instead, I'd like to explore sex's purpose in your marriage in *full light of the gospel* and subsequently provide three parameters for glorifying God through sex. The details are best left up to you! If you're equipped with an accurate biblical understanding of sex, you can apply that wisdom for a lifetime of enjoyment and improvement.

The Purposes of Sex and Intimacy

The first step toward understanding God's purpose for sex is acknowledging that he made it, and everything God makes is good! Just a few decades ago, such an understanding was revolutionary. Today, you probably agree, so we'll move right along. (If you don't agree, keep reading anyway.)

One of the first directives God gave Adam and Eve was to go forth and multiply—to fill the earth (Gen. 1:28). This command, given against the backdrop of all creation, reveals God's first purpose for sex: procreation. As husband and wife are physically joined during sex, they are literally unified through the miracle of conception. Two completely independent individuals are joined at the molecular level as their DNA combines. We must recall that DNA and the processes of its replication were discovered less than a century ago. Had we written this book in the early 1900s, we couldn't have appreciated *becoming one flesh* in the same way. Today, we get to marvel at the wonder and complexity of God's design for sex and, even more so, how he has graciously allowed us to play a role in co-creating new life.

When a couple has sex, a completely new flesh is created, but more than that, a new soul is conceived. In Genesis 2, God ordains and blesses the man and his wife as they become one flesh. Then, in the next verse they're "naked and not ashamed," alluding to the act of sex and the consummation of their marriage without the blemish of sin. When we fulfill God's command to multiply, we participate in creation and profoundly reflect his image in doing so.

The second purpose of sex is unity. The words "one flesh" used in Genesis were both literal and figurative. Just as through sex DNA strands are merged to create new life, the act of sex spiritually merges husband and wife. As a unified flesh, spouses are commanded to love each other as they would love themselves. The apostle Paul emphasized this profound truth when he instructed the Ephesian church on marriage:

> In the same way husbands should love their wives as their own bodies. He who loves his wife loves himself. For no one ever hated his own flesh, but nourishes and cherishes it, just as Christ does the church. (Eph. 5:28–29)

Loving each other through the act of sex is a physical representation of the spiritual love, nakedness, and self-sacrifice spouses are called to express. During intimacy, each spouse serves and takes great pleasure in the other. Both give entirely of themselves—naked and unashamed—for the enjoyment of the other and to partake of pleasure.

Your nakedness symbolizes your vulnerability of heart and soul. Just as you love and enjoy each other's bodies, imperfections and all, you are reminded to love each other's souls with transparency and joy. Just as you comingle your bodies—your flesh—your souls are comingled. Each spouse's desire becomes the other's, their burdens are shared, and their joys are one. When a married couple engages in sex, both spouses are reminded that they are totally exposed, fully known, and *still* completely loved.

The third and most profound purpose of sex is to point us to the gospel. That might sound like an overspiritualization, but let me explain. Genesis 2:24 says, "Therefore a man shall leave his father and his mother and hold fast to his wife, and they shall become one flesh." Sex and the offspring it produces are also declarative. The Hebrew word used for flesh is *levasar*, which stems from the root word *basar*. *Basar* means to bear good tidings or *to proclaim good news.* When a devoted married couple engages in sex, they are proclaiming and declaring the good news of the gospel to each other, saying to the other, "I love you just as the perfect, eternal God, who fully knows you, your sin, and your flaws, *still* loves and pursues you despite your imperfections." It's a reminder that they're known, accepted, and loved by each other and, most importantly, by God. If and when children are produced, they also proclaim God's goodness and grace (Ps. 127:3).

The act of sex—becoming one flesh spiritually, emotionally, and physically—is also a foreshadowing of the church's ultimate union with God, the final marriage of Christ and his Bride. Timothy Keller writes, "Sex is for fully committed relationships because it is to be a foretaste of the joy that comes from being in complete union with God. The most rapturous love between a man and woman is only a hint of God's love for us."[1]

Paul clearly understood this principle, as shown in his exhortation to the husbands and wives of Ephesus. He even calls it a profound mystery:

> "Therefore a man shall leave his father and mother and hold fast to his wife, and the two shall become one flesh." This mystery is profound, and I am saying that it refers to Christ and the church. (Eph. 5:31–32)

When we experience the exclusive, intimate love of another through sex, it is euphoric. Every aspect of our being is *involved* with the other; we're physically and emotionally consumed by the selfless, sacrificial, naked act of love that sex represents. It's hard to imagine complete union with God. It's too lofty an idea to grasp. If Keller is right, then sex in its right context is perhaps the clearest glimpse of what it will be like to love and receive love from God in perfect union unadulterated by sin.

Sex is packed with purpose. God made it, and it is great. So far we've discussed three main purposes of sex, but in what tangible ways do God's purposes change our behavior? The following passage is a great place to start:

> Drink water from your own cistern,
>   flowing water from your own well.
> Should your springs be scattered abroad,
>   streams of water in the streets?
> Let them be for yourself alone,
>   and not for strangers with you.
> Let your fountain be blessed,
>   and rejoice in the wife of your youth,
>   a lovely deer, a graceful doe.
> Let her breasts fill you at all times with delight;
>   be intoxicated always in her love. (Prov. 5:15–19)

Solomon urges readers to revere and protect their intimate lives in order to enjoy them to the fullest. The best imaginable sex is available to every married couple because it is only within marriage that one finds the place, passion, and purity necessary for God-blessed sexuality.

The Place for Sex: Drink Water from Your Own Cistern

God desires for us to enjoy sex to the fullest, which is why he designed sex for the exclusivity of marriage. Solomon warns against adultery (or any sex outside marriage) by likening sex to a water source—namely, a cistern and a well.

It's an apt analogy, as sex is meant to be deep and life-giving in its proper context.

To steal from another's well is a crime, and to spill its water onto the streets is foolish and unsanitary. In ancient cultures like Solomon's, streets were much more than places for travel and commerce. They were catchall basins for trash, animal waste, human waste, and building runoff. In short, they represented the worst part of a community. It would have been unthinkable to drink water off the street, as it would have led to certain illness or even death. It would have also been unthinkable to squander one's water supply by dumping it onto the streets. Finally, sharing one's cistern or well unscrupulously would have contaminated the water. Use by livestock, coupled with washing and cleaning activities, would have deposited bacteria and parasites that would make the water undrinkable.

Within marriage, your sex life—your intimacy—is like a clean, fresh water supply. You own it; it's yours alone and "not for strangers with you." You are free to drink from your well and enjoy pure, clean water whenever you desire. Protect your well, enjoy it, and own it wholeheartedly.

How does the exclusivity of marriage—the privacy of your well—help fulfill God's purposes in your life? I can't emphasize this enough: sex in marriage is infinitely more than a physical act. It is the deepest possible expression of a spiritual covenant—a lifelong commitment to another soul, consummated by the physical joining of flesh. Solomon later warns us not to "stir up or awaken love before it pleases" (Song of Songs 2:7). To partake in the intimacy of sex without the intimacy of soul is to experience that which isn't yours. But within the covenant of marriage, you are free to run wild with each other. You are liberated to "drink water from your own cistern" and to "be intoxicated, always in her love." God doesn't just tolerate passionate sex; he encourages it! And the primary way God encourages the best possible sex is by lovingly instructing us to keep it within the confines of marriage.

Finally, God's divine purposes for sex can only be accomplished within the context of biblical covenant between spouses. Through sex, children are created, and within a household founded on covenant, they flourish. Countless studies prove the same. Becoming one flesh physically is fueled by becoming one flesh spiritually. Sex without the lifelong, selfless love of covenant is without purpose; it is selfish. Sex within covenant melds two bodies and souls together in a radical display of intimacy, service, and oneness on every level. Finally, the relentless love of God in the gospel is reflected most when two imperfect individuals submit to and are bound by a covenant that transcends themselves. If sex is a foreshadowing of our forever, perfect unity with Christ as his Bride, then sex's only appropriate context is a lifelong covenant where each party is loved with boundless grace and with spiritual sanctification as their ultimate prize.

If you're reading this as an engaged or single person, I encourage you to abstain from sex until you're married for the above reasons. Two adults who have sex outside of marriage should not expect to experience the fullness of joy available—even if they're on track for marriage. Premarital sex is a sin, and like all sin, it dishonors God and robs us of the complete joy he adamantly desires for us. If you've already had sex outside of marriage, you need only turn to Jesus and earnestly repent. God's grace is sufficient to redeem your married sex life so it reflects his desire, fulfills his purposes, and maximizes your joy.

Additionally, any activity that breaks the exclusivity of sex in marriage should be avidly avoided. We've been asked if viewing pornography with your spouse as a means for sexual arousal is acceptable, and our answer is always a resounding no. Pornography is a perversion of God's design, and bringing it into your marriage—or any aspect of your life—is never acceptable.

The Purity of Sex: Let Your Fountain Be Blessed

Many couples have asked us about what's permissible in the bedroom. What's okay and what's off-limits? You may have wondered the same; I know we have. Such questions are natural. It's common for one spouse to feel more adventurous in bed than the other spouse. This can lead to frustration, anxiety, and even shame if it's not addressed with love and discernment.

Much of the confusion about what's *allowed* during sex is due to our cultural context. Cultural perversions—distortions—of sexuality can lead to unhealthy expectations toward each other, discontentment, and shame. The clearest example is pornography, which has distorted many people's views about what they will experience—what they *should* experience—with their spouse during intimacy.

As disciples of Christ, we must remain watchful and seek clarity and unity in the bedroom. We must guard our wells and keep them pure by allowing the gospel to transform our minds, motivate our agendas, and inform the sexual experience. While no single biblical text gives us a list of sexual dos and don'ts, Scripture provides many examples of selfless love that help us discern what's good, pure, and wise for building intimacy.

Hebrews 13:4 instructs us to "let the marriage bed be undefiled"—set apart, different, special. In other words, even within marriage, we must keep sex holy if it is to fulfill the purposes for which it was designed.

Let's take a broader view. If the ultimate purpose of marriage is to reflect the covenant love between Christ and the church, and if sexual intimacy is a physical expression of that unifying love between spouses, then *everything about sex should align with the attitudes of love*. Love and purity go hand in hand. Love wouldn't encourage another to sin, love wouldn't ask the other to perform degrading or painful acts, and love wouldn't breach the exclusivity and sanctity of the marriage bed. Love wouldn't ask another to violate their conscience. Lust, on the other hand, would.

To further contrast, consider these comparisons of love versus lust:

- Lust is self-serving; love is selfless.
- Lust prefers the body first; love values the soul above all else.
- Lust is shortsighted; love works with eternity in view.
- Lust is foolish; love is wise.
- Lust rushes; love is patient.
- Lust treats a person as an object to be used; love treats a person as a soul to be cherished.
- Lust is lazy; love is diligent.
- Lust is poison; love is pure.

One need only read 1 Corinthians 13 to see the characteristics of love clearly defined. Love is patient, gentle, kind, selfless, and "does not insist on its own way" (1 Cor. 13:5). Some sexual acts, while permissible according to Scripture, may not be beneficial because they are motivated by selfishness. Even permissible acts become degrading if one spouse is coercing or forcing the other to perform them. Selfishness spoils true intimacy every time.

The key to maintaining purity in intimacy is to nurture a right view of sex and emphasize its role in fulfilling God's purposes for your marriage: to bind you as one flesh spiritually and physically, and to reflect the gospel. Any act that exhibits and reinforces selfless, covenant love is permissible during sex, and any act that contradicts it is not.

The details are best left up to you and your spouse.

The Passion of Sex: Be Intoxicated Always in Her Love

The place and purity of your sexual relationship set the stage for the main act: passion. In the final verse of the passage above, Solomon suddenly drops the metaphor and shifts his language in dramatic fashion. You can feel the momentum build as his passion mounts: "Let her breasts fill you at all times with delight; be intoxicated always in her love" (Prov. 5:19). His abruptness should invite questions in us. Why is *intoxication* the next natural step after drinking of "your own well"? In one verse he's talking about fountains, and the next, breasts? Talk about cutting to the chase. Why is that?

Throughout Scripture, nakedness usually refers to shame, disgrace, and judgment (Gen. 3:7; Isa. 47:3; Lam. 1:8), but not here. Here, in this place (marriage), with this intent (pure motivations), nakedness only emboldens lovers. It enlivens and liberates them. It is as if they are finally free of their restraints; at last they're allowed to drink deep of their well and revel in its purity until they're utterly satisfied. The Song of Solomon is rife with vivid dialogue and imagery where the young lovers are naked, unashamed, and lost in passionate pursuit. God created sex to be a passionate exchange. Nothing about it is shocking to him.

Selena and I were both virgins on our wedding night. We always knew we wanted to save sex for the day we were married, but it wasn't easy. To be honest, our desire to have sex was one of the main reasons we got married at twenty and twenty-one years old. It was a constant, losing battle, so I sold my car and bought a ring (no joke). Had we been able to restrain ourselves, we would have probably finished college first and saved ourselves some heartache! However, our hormone-fueled passion was a leviathan on a leash made of twine. It was only a matter of time until it broke loose.

We struggled for years to keep our physical passion on hold, and I can't lie: it was *horrible*. Just the worst. While we got married as virgins, we had plenty of moments when we went further than we should have. Our passion often got the better of us, and it was always accompanied by regret, guilt, and shame. We knew in our hearts that anywhere outside the covenant of marriage wasn't the right place to indulge in sexual intimacy. We always had to hold back. I can't tell you how many times I abruptly got up off the couch and just left without saying a word. No matter how passionate our make-out sessions got, it never felt right. At least, not until our wedding night. That night, *that* night. Well, wow.

I honestly don't know how to describe it. It was as if in a single moment, God lifted the Hoover Dam from its footings and the full force of the Colorado River burst forth. Our passion had a place. The leviathan had been unleashed. Nothing could stop it, and nothing *should*. It was right and good—finally! We were at last within God's design, free to be naked *and* unashamed, to touch each other without guilt, to drink deep of *our* well in its right place and with the purity God desired. Now, don't get me wrong; we were both very naïve about sex. We had *lots* to learn about loving each other well in a brand-new way. So we soberly resolved to practice as much possible. It was the least we could do.

Learning to Love . . . in Bed

You're never more vulnerable than when you're naked and close to each other. All of your imperfections are on display. When you're naked physically together, you both have opportunities to love and be loved as you are. Vulnerability is good and worth pursuing in this context, but it can also create confusion and cause frustration. You're both sinners saved by grace. The same grace is necessary as you learn to love each other sexually. It's a journey, your journey, and it will take time to learn how to navigate.

Covenant marriage provides the perfect context for sexual expression and exploration, but sometimes you need help. That's okay. If you feel like your sex life isn't all you'd hoped for, take a deep breath and relax. You're not the first and you won't be the last. You have a lifetime to figure each other out. Sex will get better as you learn your spouse and their desires. This is the amazing relief of God's design for marriage: you have the same person to love for your entire life. You get to grow in your intimacy with each other emotionally, spiritually, and *sexually*.

Sex can be a tough topic, and we don't mean to paint with too broad a brush. However, in our years of helping married couples, we've realized thematic pain points that affect most couples. The ability to be vulnerable, asymmetrical desire, communication, and expectations all play roles in intimacy. It can take years of work and counseling to resolve deep sexual problems and root out their causes. Nothing will replace godly counsel and gospel-centered community to help you heal and grow; be sure to seek out both.

So far we've discussed God's design for sex, explored its purposes, and outlined its parameters. By now you've hopefully gained an understanding of underlying principles that should fuel behavior. With that understanding, we can now explore healthy, practical ways to *improve* your sex life as a married couple. Here are some ideas and tools to help you venture further together and kindle a mutually honoring, healthy, and passionate sex life. Selena will start by discussing a topic she's grown in personally: sexual vulnerability.

Embracing Vulnerability

SELENA

I am so incredibly thankful for my husband's perspective on sex and intimacy both now and before we got married. We fought fiercely to save sex for our wedding night, and when it finally arrived, I was woefully naïve. We *both* were. My expectations were met in ways I didn't anticipate, and overall I'd say our honeymoon was a great experience. But if I were to compare our sex life then to now, it's only gotten richer over time as we've learned to love each other more completely and with greater vulnerability.

As Ryan mentioned, sex is *so much more* than a physical experience, but that wasn't the perspective I brought into our marriage. There were many times early on when I thought, *This is it? This is sex; this is what Ryan and I will do for years to come.* I had no idea the depth and beauty that existed in the physical act of sex. It wasn't until I began to understand the gospel that I began to grasp the roles of sex beyond the physical.

My perspective of sex and intimacy was limited by deep personal fears that made it difficult for me to be fully known and fully loved by my husband. Namely, I came from a divorced home. I grew up trying to mask myself and compensate for my broken family. My mom is amazing, and she's done so much with so little, but money was always a struggle. I also feared whenever friends would ask about my dad. What would I say? He wasn't around as often as I made it seem. I was afraid of rejection because of my lack. I spent my teenage years building an elaborate façade so people would accept me. I didn't realize it, but I carried this same fear of rejection into our marriage. My fear kept Ryan at arm's length, especially in the bedroom.

Everything changed when I experienced real, unconditional love for the first time through my good friend Rachel. I had sinned against her. She did something I disapproved of, and instead of going to her, I judged her behind her back—vocally, to other people. (It pains me to write this.) Rachel found out somehow and we were confronted with this awkward moment when I knew I needed to repent and apologize. I assumed we'd go through the motions of forgiveness, but ultimately, I'd lose a friend. Thankfully, I was wrong.

After I apologized and asked for forgiveness, Rachel graciously and generously spoke these words that changed my heart forever: "Oh, Sel, there's nothing we can't get through." Her reply was like water to my parched soul. Her confident resolve in our friendship blew my mind. *How could she be so honest and transparent?* I had hurt her and let her down. She had no reason to continue our friendship—she had seen my ugly. Metaphorically speaking, I was standing there "naked" with all my sin showing, and she lovingly showed me Jesus in return.

Right then, I realized that my fear of vulnerability had only kept me alone and shallow; it didn't keep me safe like I thought. Hiding only hinders intimacy, but vulnerability met with gospel-motivated love always produces confident closeness.

Intimacy in marriage is a glimpse of the type of vulnerability available in Christ. When you're exposed and naked with your spouse physically, it is a symbol of the reciprocal vulnerability you are called to experience on every level. I've since learned to embrace vulnerability in sex. If we settle for anything short of total exposure, we risk missing out on the freedom, security, and joy available to marriages built on Christ.

Asymmetrical Desire

RYAN

Vulnerability is a necessity during intimacy, but what if you don't desire sex equally? What if there aren't enough opportunities for sexual vulnerability? This part's for you.

Selena and I don't naturally have the same appetite for sex. Few couples do. Maybe you're in the minority of couples who share identical sex drives, and if so—congratulations! I say that with sincerity; you're blessed in a very unique way. If you don't share the same desire for sex, we know your pain. I'll call this asymmetrical desire: where one spouse naturally wants more sex than the other.

Our asymmetrical desire for sex grew into resentment between us. Not just frustration, *resentment*. I brought expectations into our marriage that neither of us knew existed until years in. I'd often feel neglected and deprived if we didn't have sex when I expected it, which led to emotional bitterness and an eventual shutdown of communication. Selena felt obligated to give me sex (which decimates intimacy), and it caused her to build walls and keep me at an emotional arm's length. To make matters worse, her fear of disappointing me was exacerbated by my sexual frustration. It was a relentless cycle that went on for years. She felt like a bad wife, and I felt like an unlovable, unwanted husband. Sex had become a huge, festering issue in our marriage, and instead of building intimacy between us it was driving us further and further apart.

Lights On, Windows and Doors Wide Open

That went on until my friend Shawn showed me how to live with radical transparency. One day, while we were hiking, he explained to me how freedom and integrity are readily available to those who hide nothing—or, as he puts it, those who live with "lights on, windows and doors wide open." It wasn't just an idea for Shawn; he *actually lived this way* and it was obvious. It was also ridiculous. I thought, *How can I possibly live like that?* But I knew I wanted—*I needed*—what he had. Selena and I needed to live transparently. I needed to be guided by integrity and root out destructive duplicity in our marriage (Prov. 11:3 NIV).

That was when Selena and I learned the power of *truly* honest conversations and began having them. As a result, we began to heal. We talked about our struggles. I repented of lust rooted in bitterness, she repented of being driven by fear, and we articulated for the first time a path toward intentional intimacy. Just by talking we were able to align our expectations, live more transparently, meet each other in the middle, and, in turn, begin experiencing deeper intimacy. Christ guided us every step of the way as we pressed into our identities in him. We are both sinners saved by grace; how could we expect each other to be perfect? Only Christ is perfect, but in him we finally found the freedom to hide no longer—to be honest and vulnerable with one another, to forgive, and to pursue each other *despite* our imperfections just as he has loved and pursued us (Rom. 5:8).

Perhaps the most valuable outcome of living and communicating transparently is that neither of us had to guess what the other was thinking; we needed only to ask. I made Selena a simple promise that forever changed our communication: she could ask me anything, and I would never lie or sugarcoat the truth. This was the first step toward rebuilding trust and vulnerability between us.

Throughout our reconciliation and repenting, we shared countless words, big tears, long silences, and prayers. Our newfound transparency opened fresh opportunities for intimacy. Every topic was fair game; every concern, frustration, joy, shameful moment, and random thought was worthy of conversation. Slowly, our communication was revolutionized as God continued working in our hearts. We could now discuss our expectations and diffuse frustration without running the emotional minefield or risking a heated argument. We cleared the air, and unity was our common objective. Our expectations were finally out in the open and they began to align as we sought to love and know each other more intentionally.

Aligning Expectations

I love talking with young engaged couples. I enjoy the unabashed enthusiasm and bravado with which they approach their impending sex lives together. We've often shared our story with them, not to taper or lessen their expectations for sex but rather to help them gain agreement and enter their own marriage with both eyes wide open. Here's the reality: married sex has more potential for passion than you ever imagined but it will require more intentionality than you ever anticipated.

Every couple brings to their marriage a mixed bag of sexual expectations. Most expectations fall into one of three buckets: sex's role, importance, and ability to fulfill needs; its frequency, or how often they will have it; and what the sexual experience will entail. Candid conversations are necessary to address and align your expectations in each area. Have them! Below are three tools we've found illuminating and helpful for starting honest conversations about expectations and sex.

Keeping Perspective

We've spent the bulk of this chapter discussing God's design and purposes for sex. Indeed, it is a profound blessing and responsibility! However, it's good to nuance our understanding at this point in the conversation. Fulfilling sex in marriage is not an end in itself to be pursued; it is a result of a loving covenant and deep spiritual intimacy. If we place too much weight on the importance of sex as an end to be pursued itself, we create an idol that can (and will) fail. When you struggle to connect sexually, it can feel like your relationship is falling apart. In reality, the act of sex represents a small fraction of your life together.

Scott Kedersha, a marriage pastor in Texas, shared an interesting insight with me. He has spent years counseling, teaching, and mentoring countless couples before and during marriage. He told me that the average couple spends just 0.625 percent of their married lives having sex. I was shocked to hear such a low number, but after breaking it down, it makes sense. According to Scott, the average couple has sex about six times per month. If each session lasts forty-five minutes, they will spend a total of 270 minutes, or four and a half hours, having sex every thirty days. That sounds like a significant amount, but as the average month has 720 hours, its magnitude is quickly put in perspective.

Again, that's an average amount. You could be on either side of that number, but the point remains: the activity of sex represents a small fraction of your married life together. I say this not to diminish the value of sexual intimacy (this whole chapter is devoted to saying otherwise) but rather to help provide perspective. Marriage is a vast, complex endeavor. Your sexual experience is an indicator of something greater than just sex itself. It's like a highlight reel. Your sex life will evolve as your spiritual and emotional intimacy grows, and that's a good thing. It's important not to lose heart if and when sexual frustration sets in and to remember that you can and *will* persevere through dry spells.

Sex is important but it isn't everything. It's a small part of the larger picture, so if you're feeling frustrated you are free to relax in the knowledge that you're both constant works in progress. Focus on pursuing each other's hearts and souls. Press through and talk. Let your soul-intimacy set the stage for your sexual experience, and guard against allowing the activity of sex to hinder your intimacy outside the bedroom.

The Spectrum of Sex

One of our candid conversations has produced what we call "the spectrum of sex." We realized that we have different modes of sexual intimacy. Sometimes it's fast and functional, other times it's slow and rapturous. It's like comparing a Ferrari to a freight train. The Ferrari is fast and flashy; it travels from A to B as quickly as possible and can stop on a dime. A freight train takes much longer to gain momentum and reach its final destination, and once it gets going, good luck stopping it!

We've discovered that it's helpful to get on the same page as quickly as possible by identifying what mode of sex we're shooting for—or where we're at on the spectrum at that moment. Life is busy, Selena chases our kids around the house, and there are countless items on both our to-do lists. Those are great times to take the Ferrari for a spin. Other times, we plan. We *book a trip*, if you will. We drop the kids off at their grandparents' house, schedule dinner, talk, laugh, and go for a long ride on the evening train . . . if you catch my drift.

Prior to understanding our spectrum of sex, we would often miss each other's expectations, and our attempts at intimacy would end in an argument. Now we have a fast way to articulate our individual expectations. If ever they're not aligned, we talk through it and find a healthy compromise.

By candidly discussing your expectations in the moment you can quickly get on the same page. Do you have a spectrum of sex in your marriage? Find conversation primers that work for you, and in all things, communicate.

Find Your Rhythm (No Pun Intended)

Many couples ask us how often they should be having sex to stay healthy. It would be unwise to prescribe or recommend that you have sex every so-and-so number of days, or X number of times per week. No two couples are the same. I encourage you to honestly discuss your individual sexual needs. About how long does it take for each of you to begin desiring sex after you've had it? How often do you need the full "freight train" experience and how often will the Ferrari suffice? What are your physiological needs as a man or as a woman? What has worked best for your relationship in the past? What's realistic given your current stage in life?

Selena and I have discovered that we need a certain amount of sex to keep us connected and functioning in unity. After years of trial and error, we've arrived at two to three times per week as our optimal frequency. Having this rough figure in mind helps us in various ways.

First, it creates a natural life rhythm that indicates to us both when we're due for some intimate time. Doing so removes surprise and mystery from the equation. She's never surprised when day three rolls around, and I'm rarely wondering when it will be a good time to *put out the vibe*. Both of us enjoy the predictability, albeit for different reasons.

181

Second, knowing our rhythm helps us take better advantage of opportunities when they arise. It sounds counterintuitive, but we're actually more spontaneous now that we have a target frequency in mind. Having young children can make maintaining a healthy sex life exceedingly difficult. In daily life there might be an unexpected thirty-minute period when both kids are napping and we're working on something. We've found ourselves in those moments when we both simultaneously look over our laptop screens at each other and signal with our eyes, *Are you thinking what I'm thinking?* Off we go! Totally unexpected. The same is true if we're headed into a busy few days or if one of us is headed out of town. We know that if a trip will last more than a few days, it's healthiest for us to make time for sex just before leaving and immediately upon returning.

The goal behind finding your ideal rhythm and frequency is to align your expectations and make each other a priority. It also clearly delineates when you and your spouse are likely to need sex both physiologically and emotionally. Having a mutual understanding will help you apply Paul's instructions to Corinthian husbands and wives:

> Do not deprive one another, except perhaps by agreement for a limited time, that you may devote yourselves to prayer; but then come together again, so that Satan may not tempt you because of your lack of self-control. (1 Cor. 7:5)

Sexual deprivation is never ideal unless it's intentional and agreed upon. Paul understood that couples need regular access to each other. The same is still true today. Selena and I have unwittingly deprived each other of sex in the past just by having misaligned expectations. Seek agreement in your expectations by finding the frequency and modes that work best for you.

Go Forth in Freedom

Sex is an awesome gift and a rich blessing, one crafted in the hands of God himself. It's a holy endeavor worthy of your attention, time, and effort. Sex is designed by God for his purposes, your enjoyment, and, ultimately, his glory.

Passionate sex is a natural byproduct of intimacy on every level. But the most fulfilling passion is only possible in full light of God's purposes for sex, in the right place, and with love-fueled purity. In the proper context, your nakedness is without shame and your passion is without restraint. A fire set in the wild will scorch entire forests, but fire kindled on the hearth of your home will burn with life-giving warmth. If the parameters of place and purity are present, let your passion run free. Have fun, enjoy yourselves, and, in doing so, honor God well.

FOR REFLECTION

- How has sex with your spouse been challenging?
- How has sex been liberating and unifying?
- Review the love versus lust list on page 169. Is there an area in your marriage where lust is the motivation?
- How can each of you take a step toward selflessly loving and giving of yourself to the other?

9

Dealing with Discord

Ground Rules for Fighting Fair and Growing through Conflict

Conflicts bring experience, and experience brings
that growth in grace which is not to be attained
by any other means.

Charles H. Spurgeon

SELENA

Returning from Switzerland after Ryan's heart surgery was
one of the most challenging seasons of our marriage. His
body had been cut open and his life was sustained through
a bypass machine—it changes a person. He was still my
husband, but with much more animosity toward God and
less patience for me and our life status at that point. Our
relationship felt burdensome on every front. Daily conversations about life became major points of contention. This once

romantic, adventurous relationship felt dry, with a constant tone of discontentment behind everything we did and said. We were slow to resolve our fights, and there were times I questioned whether or not we would be able to reconcile. I remember thinking, *Well, this is the commitment I made—in sickness and in health. God, please help me to be patient with him and love him, but please don't let this last too long.* It was a lonely place to be—distant, disconnected. I didn't ask anyone for help, because I didn't want to be transparent with them for fear of what they might see or think of us in our mess. To be honest, I was ready to settle for this being our new normal. Thankfully, God didn't let our story end there.

Let's face it: conflict in marriage is inevitable. Living face-to-face for life with another human being provides countless opportunities for conflict, no matter how good your relationship is. Ryan is my best friend, and we still experience conflicts *very* often. Our insecurities and pride rise up and it becomes the clash of the titans. In the heat of battle our goals become twisted. Instead of seeking understanding, we each get further and further entrenched in our positions. Then the fight becomes more about being right than actually dealing with whatever issue started the argument in the first place.

It's taken us years to appreciate and embrace healthy conflict. This probably sounds counterintuitive, but conflict is one of the main ways Ryan and I have grown closer. It's amid the struggle that God sanctifies the human heart. As God's people we're not unlike the Israelites being delivered from Egypt. In Christ we've been set free from death and slavery and we're headed for an ultimate promised land, but there's quite a bit of desert before we get there. The desert is where we learn to trust God, it's where we learn to hear from him, and it's where we learn how to obey him wholeheartedly.

Conflicts in marriage are like deserts. As we traverse, we often find ourselves parched and hungry, tired and hopeless, but that is because we've failed to trust God completely and find everything we need in him. We've been delivered and called God's own and we have eternal hope in God's promises. Until then, we're being made holy. Somewhere between hope and deliverance lies *sanctification.*

The road to sanctification is lined with conflict—with ourselves, our spouses, and our circumstances. But God is faithful to sustain us the entire way. No circumstance or failure can remove his claim on our lives. God has been faithful to soften my heart and show me how to have peace in the middle of our conflicts. He has taught me to trust. He has shown me the difference between being right and being loving. He's taught me that the weight and burden of real resolution rests on Christ alone. Yes, we're called to co-labor with Christ—to work through every conflict as a couple— but ultimately, we can only reconcile because *we have been reconciled to Christ.*

We can only love because we are loved.

And we can only forgive because we have experienced radical forgiveness ourselves.

True and lasting reconciliation with our spouses, like every aspect of marriage, *begins* and *ends* with Jesus.

Shallow Answers to Deep Problems

Over the years, Ryan and I have received thousands of messages from people whose marriages have been destroyed by conflict, usually because of unrepented sin rooted in a heart that's hardened toward both God and spouse. As previously mentioned, postsurgery Ryan was not the same Ryan with whom I had said "I do" two years prior.

We felt like our faith was strong and we believed that God had brought us through it all and that Ryan was a miracle. But we still wrestled with the *why*. We asked ourselves, *Is God punishing us for leaving on such a whim?* Having gone on this European adventure only to be humbly brought back to our hometown in the States, broke, looking for jobs and feeling ashamed—we felt the situation invited the question. Looking back, I believe that the ground of our two-year-old marriage was beginning to harden. The newness was wearing off and familiarity was setting in. Our relationship post-Switzerland felt dry and stiff with discontentment. Conflict after conflict after conflict—it seemed we couldn't catch a break, and although we felt like we were clinging to God, we functioned as if we didn't have a Savior.

Keeping our hearts soft when our whole life together was an obvious mess to everyone else was tough, but it forced us to deal with our pride and insecurities. Too many times I let my pride take the lead. I'd put a smile on my face when all the while my heart was tired, hard, and angry toward Ryan and our life together. Insecurity brought on fear that fueled my not-so-wise decision making. Our communication was unintentional and sometimes nonexistent (the silent treatment). We could hardly agree on anything, which meant our evenings typically ended in a charged yelling match or me in tears. Sometimes it seemed easier to ignore whatever the conflict was between us and just hope it would go away.

Praise God, he led us through and used the conflicts we were facing to bring us back, first to him and then to each other. It's by his grace, and our tenacity to fight for each other even when we didn't feel like it, that we are still married today. Thankfully we were both taught the power of repentance and forgiveness at a very young age, and they have been a large part of our relationship since the beginning. In the moments when it seemed easier to ignore the conflict or blow it off and not deal with problems we were facing (short fuses, pride, anger, lack of respect, pursuing our own desires without considering the other, and so on), we couldn't ignore the deep convictions from the Holy Spirit. There was a longing for reconciliation with each other that was deeper than our need to be right.

There were times when we simply had to grit our teeth, cling to God's Word, and seek authentic forgiveness from each other. This continual cycle of repenting and forgiving kept our hearts soft toward God and each other. Instead of fighting with Ryan, I started to fight for him by learning how to be painfully honest and transparent—trusting God and taking him at his Word. It was not fun showing off my hard heart to Ryan and repenting of my prideful moments, but God knew that without repentance and forgiveness in our marriage, we were headed for disaster. The fact is, conflict takes on many shapes and forms, and whatever or whoever is at the core of our marriage will ultimately determine our response.

Obviously no married couple plans for this. Every couple enters marriage hoping for the best, but sin creeps in like the serpent in the garden and causes us to question God and his goodness. It's the small voice in our ears telling us that God got it wrong, we have the solution, and it's up to us to fix what he broke. All too often our conflicts begin when our belief in God, at some level, waivers. Our heart hardens toward his Word because we think we know better. This leads us to stray outside our covenant boundaries into unprotected territory.

So how do we deal with conflict in our marriage? What does God's Word say about divorce? In order to really address these questions and bring clarity and guidance, we must look to Jesus first.

In the early years of our marriage we didn't understand how to deal with conflict in a biblical way. When we asked our trusted friends at the time, we were given shallow, trite, quick-fix responses of either how to avoid conflict or how to look to ourselves for answers.

So often resolution to our problems meant my giving in and letting Ryan be right or get his way. Instead of compromising out of love for one another, we compromised out of selfishness. I was tired of fighting and desperate for joy; I longed for any semblance of happiness, shallow or not. It was easier to be indifferent and just move on in hopes that *somehow* things would change.

The world is quick to offer prescriptive answers. There is no shortage of marital advice available to those who seek it, such as "Five Tips for Better Communication," or "Ten Ways to Rekindle the Fire in Your Sex Life." The internet is riddled with messages of inner-power and self-help, all aimed at fixing widely felt marital needs.

Try harder! Do more! Change your mindset! Worldly wisdom tells us we can be our own god and the commander of our own destinies. The allure is strong; after all, it appeals to the very core of our sin nature: a desire for independence from God. If we just pull ourselves up by our bootstraps and if we try hard enough, then we can master areas of conflict in our marriage.

Despite our best efforts, Ryan and I *never* found a perfect solution. Nor did we find peace from the conflict our marriage was facing until we *first* understood the depth of our own sin and need for Jesus. We *need* him. Jesus is not just a means to a better life; he *is* the better life.

In Christ, every fight, argument, communication issue, and struggle becomes an opportunity for us to experience his intervening grace and unrelenting love. Without him, all the effort and striving in the world won't work. Christ is every answer.

Jesus: Our Savior and Answer

I do have one caveat: if we're not careful, "Jesus is the answer" just becomes another trite, quick-fix phrase. If you're anything like me you've probably asked yourself, *How* exactly *is Jesus the answer? How does knowing I'm sinful and Jesus is perfect* actually *help my marriage?* I'm glad you asked.

Paul wrote a letter to the Colossians addressing sinful tendencies and behaviors they carried over into their new life with Christ. They were God's people, sealed by the blood of Christ—and they were forgetful. Sound familiar? He reminds them who they are *because* of Jesus:

> If then you have been raised with Christ, seek the things that are above, where Christ is, seated at the right hand of God. Set your minds on things that are above, not on things that are on earth. For you have died, and your life is hidden with

Christ in God. When Christ who is your life appears, then you also will appear with him in glory.

Put to death therefore what is earthly in you: sexual immorality, impurity, passion, evil desire, and covetousness, which is idolatry. (Col. 3:1–5)

Being "raised with Christ" implies death with Christ. Our new life in Jesus means our selfish, sinful selves have died, or lost the power to rule us, on the cross. "We know that our old self was crucified with him in order that the body of sin might be brought to nothing, so that we would no longer be enslaved to sin" (Rom. 6:6). We are living sacrifices (12:1), called to die to our old self daily. Over a century ago, evangelist D. L. Moody said, "The problem with a living sacrifice is that it keeps crawling off the altar."[1] You will never feel the meaning of that phrase more than in marriage. Old habits and tendencies are laid bare, and your spouse will be the first to see (and feel) them.

We must constantly die to our flesh anytime our old selves—our sinful natures—come back to life. Paul instructs us to put them to death (Col. 3:5). But how? By setting our minds on things that are above (v. 2) and living out of what Christ has accomplished on the cross as we are hidden with him (v. 3). *This* is the place where true conflict resolution begins: hidden with Christ in God. Approaching conflict from this place of being "in" or "hidden" in Christ means living honestly and openly with each other, sacrificing your feelings and trusting God's way to bring restoration and fullness.

In the first year of our marriage Ryan confessed to me that he was dealing with pornography. Whether you've been married for thirty years or one year, the impact of this confession is deep. It's hard to hear that your husband has sought pleasure with someone else. There is shame involved with both parties. As a wife, I remember thinking, *Maybe I'm not enough?* He broke my trust, which was already a challenge for me. And now he was confessing and confiding in me—he was asking me for help. I felt divided: everything in me raged with anger, hurt, and frustration, yet I was being petitioned to extend grace and forgiveness. In those moments God taught me that grace and forgiveness weren't about excusing the sin, they were about dying to my fleshly desire to yell hurtful things at him. Instead, I needed to trust and believe that I could live and respond out of the peace and security I'd been given because my life was now hidden in Christ and was not my own (Rom. 8:9). John Piper said in a podcast, "When we belong to Jesus, we're finally able to make God look glorious in our lives."[2]

Yes, my whole being felt betrayed and my feelings were hurt. But knowing that I was hidden in Christ—that I have been forgiven for much—how could I not forgive my husband? My only response to Ryan could be one of grace and forgiveness. There were still moments of anger and hurt that I had to deal with and calmly explain to Ryan. He felt the weight of that. God brought us out of Ryan's addiction to pornography through his lovingkindness. We trusted God's Word that instructs us to repent and forgive.

God faithfully rebuilt our marriage after Ryan's confession. Our trust is confident and we are each other's accountability partner. God has shown me how to be a safe harbor for my husband to securely confide in. We now deal with discord at an open and honest level that doesn't allow shame or fear to have the final say. How? By dying to the desires that would destroy each other—daily!

Dying always begins by laying your life at the foot of the cross—by looking to Jesus for satisfaction. And conflict will always point you there. It is at the end of ourselves where we learn to embrace the knowledge of Christ's great love. Because of love, God became flesh, pursued us here on earth, bore the wrath of our sin, and died so we can live (Eph. 2:1–8).

There is no truer example of love and sacrifice than in Jesus. It's out of knowing and understanding the truth and love of God in Christ that I can *finally* stop white-knuckling my own desires. I can give in—not out of exhaustion or fear but out of being deeply loved.

Can you feel that freedom? With Christ, every conflict in marriage is a gracious reminder to rest in and extend his love. When both of you understand this, your conflicts will naturally grow shorter in length and further apart in frequency.

Pursuing Your Partner

Whenever Ryan pursues me in the heat of an argument—his defenses go down and he empathizes with me or asks how he can help instead of arguing—*that's* when my defenses go down and my heart of stone is turned to mush. I feel his love through his selflessness, and instead of letting my feelings and emotions dictate my response, I am better able to do what Paul urges: to put to death what is earthly inside me. Ryan's love and security in Christ help me put my selfishness away and work *with* him toward resolution.

Maybe you're reading this and thinking, *Okay, Selena; but see, my husband never pursues me. He just always tries to win.* To you I would say: Have you tried dying to your own selfish desires and pursuing him? Remember the freedom we have in Christ. Our hearts can rest secure and satisfied because of Jesus and the hope he brings. This empowers me to listen and pursue my husband's heart even if he doesn't pursue me.

Paul goes on:

> But now you must put them all away: anger, wrath, malice, slander, and obscene talk from your mouth. Do not lie to one another, seeing that you have put off the old self with its practices and have put on the new self, which is being renewed in knowledge after the image of its creator. (Col. 3:8–10)

Dying to your old self means also putting on your new self. Paul is telling us to live out of what Jesus has done—to live in light of the gospel—by being renewed in knowledge. That's the power of being in Christ! Reality hasn't changed (arguments still happen), but our view of it is expanded. The rules of engagement have changed *because* of Christ. Suddenly, being compassionate, kind, meek, and patient somehow makes sense. In Christ we can endure problems and face trials together. We fight *for* each other instead of *with* each other. We can "bear with one another" because we need not look to each other or inside of ourselves for resolution. We can look to Jesus, in whom we are free and forgiven. Our marriage covenant is no longer a cage we're trapped in but a safe arena to work out the true, unfailing meaning of being loved by God and renewed in Christ.

Paul continues with so much more about the new self:

> Put on then, as God's chosen ones, holy and beloved, compassionate hearts, kindness, humility, meekness, and patience, bearing with one another and, if one has a complaint against

another, forgiving each other; as the Lord has forgiven you, so you also must forgive. And above all these put on love, which binds everything together in perfect harmony. And let the peace of Christ rule in your hearts, to which indeed you were called in one body. And be thankful. (vv. 12–15)

As we live in the reality of Christ, compassion and kindness more readily flow out of our hearts toward each other. Over time and through continually "bearing with one another," forgiveness and love become more natural responses. Our marriage becomes marked by Christ's otherworldly peace even amid storms because our full weight rests on the only One who can bear it: the never-ending God of the universe.

Paul ends this passage with directives to continue remembering what Jesus has done:

Let the word of Christ dwell in you richly, teaching and admonishing one another in all wisdom, singing psalms and hymns and spiritual songs, with thankfulness in your hearts to God. And whatever you do, in word or deed, do everything in the name of the Lord Jesus, giving thanks to God the Father through him. (vv. 16–17)

I have what I like to call "should prayers" in our marriage. These are prayers that I don't like to pray but I know I *should*. They typically go like this: "Jesus, please help me with the blind spots in my relationship with Ryan. Show me areas where I am selfish, prideful, and just plain ignorant. Help me to see you in these areas, and please uproot them from my heart. Show me areas where I can trust you more." It's prayers like those that will mess with your business. They usually lead to my eating very large pieces of humble pie. My pride doesn't want to ask God to show me my faults.

Why can't I just always be right? But I'm reminded: in the Christian life, death always precedes life. We die to ourselves in exchange for life in Christ. And the life Jesus gives is fuller and more abundant than we could ever imagine.

The mark of a marriage that rests in the grace of God is one in which spouses fight fiercely for biblical resolution by first seeking Jesus. It's a marriage that's transparent, open, and fearless because it is built on God. Jesus isn't a magic pill for avoiding conflict in your marriage; he's so much more. Christ is your inexhaustible source of all the hope, peace, security, strength, and love you could possibly need to fight fiercely *for* your spouse instead of *against* them.

A Guide to Fighting Fair

RYAN

When Selena and I were first married, my dad often checked in to ask me how we were doing. A few months in he asked me if we had fought yet. We were still in the thick of our honeymoon phase, so my response was a surprised and chipper one: "Nope! We're doing great!" I recall thinking how easy marriage was and not understanding what all the fuss was about. As I've mentioned, my dad's a shrink, so I found his response particularly alarming: "You're not really married until you've had your first knockdown, drag out fight." Of course he was being figurative about the "knockdown, drag out" part, but I got his point. I now see the wisdom in his words.

As Selena mentioned, fights are an inevitable result of two people spending life together. You *will* offend each other. Some offenses are minor, some are major, and others can be deal-breakers. The question is not how to *avoid* conflict but rather how to *handle* it in a healthy way. Our next question is a natural one: As people in Christ, how should we approach conflict? Believe it or not, you and your spouse aren't the first people to have disagreements. (Surprised?) Conflict is as old as civilization itself. Even Adam and Eve weren't immune, at least not after the fall. The Bible is full of instruction for handling conflict in healthy, constructive ways, which we'll definitely explore. Before we do, both spouses must agree to the following four ground rules in order to level the playing field.

Ground Rule #1: Reconciliation Is Always the Goal

Every fight should start with the same end in sight: reconciliation. Reconciliation means you're brought close again, the air is cleared, and you're fully rejoined without reservation. This is what God commands, because it's in your best interest!

You're bound by covenant, you've both promised to love, and you have nowhere to go. Fighting forever isn't an option; the fight must resolve. Agree with each other that reconciliation is always the goal.

Jesus told his followers:

> So if you are offering your gift at the altar and there remember that your brother has something against you, leave your gift there before the altar and go. First be reconciled to your brother, and then come and offer your gift. (Matt. 5:23–24)

The above passage immediately follows the Beatitudes, which makes it interesting to say the least. As we read the Beatitudes, we should feel the full weight of our imperfection.

I know I do. That's the point. Jesus is, once again, pointing us to himself. He is our only hope for ever satisfying the requirements of the law—of *perfection*. Our only cure for sin is repentance—turning away from sin and looking to Christ. Given that, when he mentions having "something against" each other and instructs us to go and be reconciled, he's saying this: don't try to atone for your offense by giving a sacrifice; go repent to the person you offended and restore your relationship.

Jesus is addressing the human heart's propensity for covering internal sin with external displays of worship. Reconciliation is only possible with repentant, willing hearts. By calling us to reconcile, Jesus ensures our hearts don't retain bitterness in order to "keep the peace" externally.

Ground Rule #2: Repentance and Forgiveness Are Nonnegotiable

There will be times when you're the offender and others when you're offended against, that much is clear. Whatever role you happen to fill, your next action is clear as well:

> Pay attention to yourselves! If your brother sins, rebuke him, and if he repents, forgive him, and if he sins against you seven times in the day, and turns to you seven times, saying, 'I repent,' you must forgive him. (Luke 17:3–4)

Rebuke is not a word often used in daily conversation, and it may make you a bit uncomfortable. It sounds like Jesus is telling us to yell self-righteously at sinners like soapbox preachers. Let's clear things up. The Greek word for rebuke, *epitimáō*, also means "admonish" or "warn to prevent something from going wrong." Jesus's command to rebuke is dealing with the heart and motivation *of the rebuker* and it's not self-righteous in the least.

To rebuke someone is to confront them honestly in love and with their well-being in mind. Think of rebuking as warning someone driving a car that they are careening toward a cliff. It's always loving to call someone out on their sin, but it must be done with a heart aimed at their very best. If your spouse sins against you, calling them on it is not only your responsibility but also the most loving thing you can do for them.

If and when you're on the sinner's side of the equation, Jesus calls you to repent—to confess—your sin to your spouse. Get it out, be honest, and don't sugarcoat it. It might be excruciating, but the last part of the passage provides all the comfort you need.

Jesus ends his statement by commanding us to forgive. Not only that, but we are to forgive without keeping track—to *no end*. It's ridiculous but it's the gospel—and in that, it's amazing. We are called to forgive each other as we are forgiven in Christ without limit, reservation, or restriction (Eph. 4:32).

Rebuke, repent, forgive, rinse, repeat. Give generous portions of grace and forgiveness to your spouse, and don't worry—you'll likely need and receive some back very soon.

Ground Rule #3: Anger Is Natural, but Never an Excuse for Sin

Selena and I often joke about her inner Hulk. She's small, but trust me, she's wiry. This is one area of our marriage where I'm exceedingly grateful for the sanctifying work of Jesus. We've had many arguments when various objects have been hurled about. It's probably more a testimony of how maddening I can be than how mad she can get, but nonetheless, there are some dishes we'll never be able to use again. I am happy to report that our dish count has stabilized over the past few years!

All humor aside, anger is a serious issue for many. There's a reason Paul warns us not to sin in our anger; he knows we're much more likely to cause damage when emotions are high. He writes: "Be angry and do not sin; do not let the sun go down on your anger, and give no opportunity to the devil" (vv. 26–27).

Anger reveals the ugliness in everyone. Of course, there are instances in Scripture of righteous anger (which is loving), but that's not what this is talking about. Paul is referring to anger that leads to actions contrary to love:

- Love is kind; anger is mean.
- Love does not boast; anger makes others feel small.
- Love is selfless; anger is selfish.
- Love soothes; anger increases pain.
- Love sees into eternity; anger can't see past its own nose.

Selena and I have often felt the nasty residual effects of sinning in our anger. I can't count the number of times I've woken up in the morning and just wanted to give her a hug but didn't feel like I could because of unresolved conflict.

It's for our own good that God commands us not to sin in anger or let the sun set on it. We've found it helpful to implement a "pause clause" in our arguments. At any point, one of us can back away from an argument with the promise that we will return to pick up the conversation at an agreed-upon date and time. This helps diffuse hot situations without abandoning timely resolution.

Ground Rule #4: Prioritize Listening and Patience

Healthy marital fighting is always an exchange. Active listening is an art, one mastered by intentionality and a desire to understand. When I get defensive I get quiet—Selena knows this. And when I get quiet it's often because I'm either thinking of what I'm going to say next or I'm stewing in my frustration. This tendency is against reconciliation, counter-Scripture, and counterproductive.

We've quoted James before, but it's good at this point to revisit his wisdom:

> Know this, my beloved brothers: let every person be quick to hear, slow to speak, slow to anger; for the anger of man does not produce the righteousness of God. (James 1:19–20)

When James instructs readers to "be quick to hear," he is saying *be eager to understand*. Instead of using your own silence to form your next arguing point, take in what your spouse is saying; process it. Ask yourself, *What's going on in my spouse's heart that is causing their frustration?*

Listening also means internalizing what someone is saying in a productive way. It's asking yourself, *How have I contributed to what they're feeling?* It's understanding that words and tone are just the tip of the iceberg and that there are miles of ice below the surface. This is only possible when you're rooted in your identity in Christ and driven by the desire to reconcile.

Next, James instructs us to be "slow to speak [and] slow to anger." He doesn't condone silence in the case of arguments! Instead, he encourages us to use intentional words. It helps to consider the inverse of James's statement: be fast to speak and fast to anger. Does that sound productive? It sounds like a recipe for regret. Sadly, we've heard from many husbands and wives who are on the receiving end of fast-speaking, fast-to-anger spouses. Fast, angry words damage trust and exploit the relationship for selfish gain. You know each other better than anyone, and because of that, you know what phrases cut the deepest. James urges against hasty, angry speaking because it's always destructive.

When you feel a conflict bubbling to the surface, remind yourself of this wisdom. Agree in advance that you'll both be quick to listen and restrained enough to use words carefully and intentionally. This is hardest to do when emotions run high, but thankfully you can look to Christ for all you need and to the Holy Spirit for timely conviction and counsel.

With that, we have our four ground rules—the playing field is officially leveled. Now let's explore a few practical methods for healthy conflict in marriage.

Fight Naked

One of the best pieces of advice we've ever received on conflict is to fight naked. Literally. It's impossible to stay mad when you're in the buff. This has proven remarkably true for us both figuratively and literally. While funny, the words "fight naked" are a tongue-in-cheek reminder of a few deep truths about conflict in marriage.

The idea of fighting naked is best understood by contrasting it with fighting with armor on. In marriage the goal is knowing and being known by your spouse; you want to experience intimacy on every level. Fighting naturally causes your defenses to go up, which can hinder honesty and vulnerability. Guarding also keeps your spouse at arm's length.

When you're naked emotionally (and/or physically), you're both able to see and be seen by the other person for who you really are. It's an intimate, trusting exchange. When you allow yourself to be seen, you're saying, "I know I'm not perfect, but I trust and want you to love me anyway." When you *see* your spouse, you see through their imperfections and remember the person you married. You can see them the way God sees them—lovable, valuable, and worth pursuing despite their imperfections.

Being "naked" also reminds you never to bring weapons into marital warfare. You can't wield a sword if you have no armor. Weapons include manipulation, coercion, hurtful speech, name calling, bringing up past mistakes, or threatening with divorce. This goes back to fighting fair. If reconciliation is your goal, then any behavior that pushes you further apart or causes intentional emotional damage to your spouse is ridiculous and unacceptable. Leave all weapons behind—or better yet, discard them for good.

In case you're wondering, the literal application of "fighting naked" works wonders as well. Every time we try it, we stop arguing and start laughing before we can even finish getting undressed. It's definitely a viable conflict resolution method for bickering and frustration in general. A lot of couples tell us that fighting well actually creates a sense of emotional closeness that can lead to, well, physical closeness. Fighting naked can save you a step.

On that note, Selena and I have actually started looking forward to makeup sex. Maybe you agree. Why is it always so great? Fighting, arguing, bickering, and selfishness always create distance between you. An intimacy void forms as you each become more entrenched. But when you reconcile, it's like a rubber band snapping back into place! This is why the hard work of true reconciliation is irreplaceable. The gap between you can only be closed by honest confrontation of sin, repentance and turning toward Jesus, and sacrificial giving to each other through listening, speaking, understanding, and empathizing in love. When you do, your affections for one another are clarified and intensified, the air is cleared, and you're free to "drink water from your own cistern" (Prov. 5:15) without reservation.

Know the Battlefield, Expose the Sin

You may be wondering, *What can we do when an offense is too deep to work through by ourselves? What if we can't do it?* Or, *What if we've tried countless times and the same offenses keep happening?* As you probably know, not all conflicts are created equal. It's important to recognize the severity and root of the issue you're dealing with. Most marital spats are temporary, resolvable results of daily coexistence. Minor conflicts like bickering, frustration, misunderstanding, and general growth pains can be addressed through healthy communication and fair fighting. However, some offenses are much graver.

Emotional and physical affairs are utterly devastating. Addiction or habitual deception, like all sin, will lead to brokenness and degradation of intimacy and trust. Emotional, spiritual, and physical abuse can leave victims feeling trapped and hopeless. There comes a point when the offense is too great or the relationship is too far gone for the couple to handle it alone. They need outside help.

The first step is recognizing that you do, in fact, need it. In our years ministering to married couples, we've realized that many hurting couples don't realize just how unhealthy their marriage is. They're too close and have experienced brokenness for too long to see their problem or foresee its inevitable end. We advise those couples to get help as soon as they can by exposing wrong behavior to a trusted, godly counselor (a therapist, pastor, mentor, or friend). Get it out in the open.

Paul explains why:

> Take no part in the unfruitful works of darkness, but instead expose them. For it is shameful even to speak of the things that they do in secret. But when anything is exposed by the light, it becomes visible, for anything that becomes visible is light. Therefore it says,
>
> > "Awake, O sleeper,
> >   and arise from the dead,
> >   and Christ will shine on you." (Eph. 5:11–14)

Expose the sin and let the full light of Christ begin the healing process. Couples who need long-term restorative care *must* have a person to walk with them—they need someone who knows their exact situation and can come alongside them in a very personal capacity.

If you're dealing with a divorce-worthy offense, don't walk through it alone. Get help. The first place we point folks is to their local church. The problem is that not all churches understand or apply the full gospel. We could share dozens of stories where couples have received false, misguided, or even heretical advice from their pastors. It's tragic and heartbreaking. Assuming you can find a Bible-based, gospel-centered church in your area, start there. They will be able to guide you and recommend healthy, safe, and productive steps forward.

If you're being physically abused, call the authorities and get yourself and your children to safety immediately. You're not obligated to enable or endure any abusive behavior in the name of marriage. You're first called to "obey God rather than men" (Acts 5:29). When discussing headship and submission, Kathy Keller says to abused wives, "A wife should not obey or aid a husband in doing things that God forbids, such as . . . abusing her. If, for example, he beats her, the 'strong help' that a wife should exercise is to love and forgive him in her heart but have him arrested." She concludes by saying, "It is never kind or loving to anyone to make it easy for him or her to do wrong."[3]

As I mentioned, some conflicts can be handled with patience and acting like adults. Others need intentional intervention from others. Don't make the mistake of trying to handle big issues without help. In most cases, as Selena will now discuss, the best outside help comes from those in your immediate community.

Community and Conflict

SELENA

Nothing replaces Christian community for dealing with marital conflict. Ryan and I have experienced firsthand the power of facing struggles in a community context. Wives help wives, husbands help husbands, and couples help couples. What a blessing to be able to go to brothers and sisters in Christ to seek new perspective and biblical wisdom.

One of my best friends helped me through a very difficult season in our lives, just before we had our first daughter. She lovingly encouraged me by saying, "Selena, something that always helps me when I'm dealing with anger and a tough situation is to give myself a short timeframe for how long I can be angry. So in this case, maybe give yourself a few days or until the end of the week to be frustrated, to cry and be angry. Then you either need to talk to this person and seek reconciliation or you let it go and give it to God." I was so blessed by this friend (who is a superhuman mom of four and a Young Life Area Director). Jesus in her is so evident and mighty. She helped me come to grips with the reality of the situation and showed me how to deal with it from a godly standpoint. Often the people we are in community with are the ones who provide the perfect encouragement and wisdom to help clear logjams from life.

Closer through Conflict

If you take one thing away from this chapter, let it be this: every conflict in marriage is an opportunity to experience God's grace in new, profound ways. Ryan and I have learned vastly more about each other through repenting and forgiving than in any other area of our marriage. That's because though sin causes brokenness, it always thrusts us to the foot of the cross. We try not to sin against each other, we hope and pray we can trust God more completely every day, but we fail. We hurt each other and we sin against God.

Like the Israelites wandering the desert, we, too, get tired and doubtful. But thank God for Jesus! Thank God his promise doesn't rely on our goodness or ability to be perfect. Thank God that he delivered us from the slavery of sin, so we don't have to live every moment under its oppression. Thank God we can experience his unrelenting, undying, inexhaustible love through Jesus. And thank God we have Jesus to help and guide us through every struggle.

Every time you hold your tongue, you can be reminded that Christ intercedes for you at the right hand of the Father (Rom. 8:34). Every time you want to walk away without resolution, you can be reminded of Christ's finished, complete work on the cross. And every time you want to quit, you can remember that Jesus will never give up on you, and we have the eternal hope of heaven that is beyond anything our human language can utter (1 Cor. 2:9).

Human covenant and human conflict go hand-in-hand, but I can't think of a better place for sanctification than within the security of marriage with my best friend by my side.

FOR REFLECTION

- When your spouse offends you, what's your initial response? How is God leading you to respond?
- Do you have a community of believers to encourage and challenge you during marital discord? If not, how will you begin finding a community?
- How has God used conflict as an opportunity to teach you?

10

Upward and Outward

Why Fighting for Your Marriage Means Fighting for the Future

God gives us of the good things of this life, not only for necessity,
   but for delight, that we may not only serve him, but serve him cheerfully.

Matthew Henry

RYAN

Chris and April had lost all hope. Like many of the couples who reach out to us for advice, their marriage was broken. They had both given up and had all but filed the divorce paperwork. Exasperated, tired, and depleted, Chris asked me point-blank, "Why is she—our marriage—even worth the effort? What are we even fighting for?" He was emotionally done, worn out by endless arguments and hurtful words. I looked him square in the eye and said, "Everything. You're fighting for everything."

It is undoubtedly true that you are called to fight to keep your marriage covenant and pursue your spouse with Christlike love. But the greater truth is that Christ is fighting on your behalf harder than you ever could.

You don't fight for your marriage as much as Christ uses your marriage to fight for you.

You don't pursue your spouse's heart as much as Christ uses your spouse to pursue your heart.

You don't prize your spouse's affection with nearly the same ferocity with which Christ prizes yours.

Every refining moment in your marriage is a reminder of God's relentless, unwavering commitment to draw you near and conform you to the image of Jesus Christ. Those moments are reminders to find all you need in Jesus and anchor your identity in him—to trust the sufficiency of what he has done instead of what you can do. That's the most exciting (albeit counterintuitive) aspect of marriage! It's not about you. It's all about Jesus. It always has been.

In our time writing to married couples, we have often asked ourselves *why*. Why should we, they, *you* fight for a stronger marriage? What's to be had on the far side of your marriage covenant—both here and now as well as when you're dead and gone?

What's the point?

We often ask ourselves those same questions. Especially when our marriage gets difficult. We're quickly entangled in the weeds of daily life. It's easy to lose sight of the grand storyline we occupy, the chief Protagonist, and our place in the plot. We must continually bend our sight upward to be reminded of exactly where we are, who we are, and of the

Author penning the script. By God's grace we know his divine intent—and we know how the story ends!

We know with forever certainty the answer to the eternal question of *why:* to sanctify God's people and reconcile Christ's Bride to him.

We don't, however, know *what* will happen between now and then. And we don't always know *how* he plans to accomplish his divine ends. Your marriage is a massive piece of God's sanctification puzzle. Your marriage is undoubtedly a primary tool in God's work to draw you and your spouse close to him. But the reason for marriage doesn't end there.

God's purposes for marriage extend inward to your heart and soul but also outward to the rest of the world.

The Commissioned Marriage

The foundational premise of this chapter is that your marriage is not only about your happiness—it's about God's eternal purpose in you and through you. Christ's work *in* your heart always extends *outward* through your hands. The fruit of gospel-centered marriage cascades into every facet of human existence. Within the marriage covenant, children flourish. By families, the church is strengthened. And through the church, communities are reached with the good news of Jesus Christ. Just as Christ is the foundation of every thriving marriage and family, thriving marriages and families are the foundation of every flourishing society.

Do we fight for healthy marriages so we can enjoy an easier existence? Do we exercise our marriage muscles in hopes of living a longer, healthier married life? Happiness is indeed a potential result of healthy marriage, but it's only part of the picture. And though those prospects are good, the larger picture is so much more exciting.

You are commissioned—called—to perpetuate the gospel through your marriage. To know and share Christ is your greatest call and your marriage's most magnificent purpose. You're probably reading this book for the betterment of your marriage here and now, but I implore you to lift your eyes also to *there* and *then*—to the distant future.

All of the glory and weight ultimately rests on Christ, but by God's grace you can participate in his work in three tangible ways: discipling future generations, building the local church, and reaching your community with the gospel.

Where Children Flourish

We're in an era of Western culture when the idea of traditional marriage is only loosely coupled with raising children. A recent Pew Research study indicates that the number of children being raised by both parents in their first marriage has decreased by more than 37 percent since the 1960s. This, while children being raised in single-parent households has nearly tripled (that's up 300 percent). Fifty years ago, births of children outside marriage were less than 10 percent of all babies born. Today, that number is greater than 40 percent. The study states, "While at one time virtually all births occurred within marriage, these two life events are now far less intertwined."[1] The reasons for these changes are complex, partially due to the rise in cohabitation and perhaps to a widespread cultural redefinition of sex, marriage, and family.

The recent upward trend of the non–nuclear family is unprecedented. There was never a time in human history when marriage between both parents played a less significant role in child raising than now. What's more alarming is how rapidly the shift occurred—over the past fifty years. Think about that for a second: the norm for all of human history has completely changed in the past fifty years! It's unprecedented. There's no way to predict exactly what will happen, but we can safely say that, as a society, we've ventured far into uncharted waters. As a married couple committed to Christ, you are called to buck the trend.

While cultural norms for raising children have changed quickly and decidedly, the Christian view remains constant. There is no better venue for children's eternal good than a Christ-centered, gospel-saturated marriage where both parents are present, engaged, and actively discipling them. As man and woman, husband and wife, father and mother, you reflect the image of God in unique, complementary ways to your kids. Your marriage is the first gospel account your children will ever witness. Through your marriage—how you love, disagree, reconcile, forgive, and sacrifice—your children can grow familiar with the gospel before ever cracking a Bible. They see a tiny glimpse of Christ's love for his Bride and a picture of the potential unity—*two becoming one*—available to them with God through redemption in Christ.

Your children will witness an image of the implicit gospel simply by watching your marriage. But they should also hear the *explicit* gospel and commands of God as you "teach them diligently to your children" (Deut. 6:7). When we discussed priorities, we established that Christ isn't just at the top of the priority list; he *is* the list. Everything in your life radiates outward from the person and work of Christ in your heart. A gospel-saturated life compels married believers to "make disciples of all nations" (Matt. 28:19), and fulfilling Christ's charge always begins in the home: spouses disciple each other, and parents disciple their children. Psalm 78 provides a clear call:

> He established a testimony in Jacob
>   and appointed a law in Israel,
> which he commanded our fathers
>   to teach to their children,
> that the next generation might know them,
>   the children yet unborn,
> and arise and tell them to their children,
>   so that they should set their hope in God
> and not forget the works of God,
>   but keep his commandments. (vv. 5–7)

I know very little about my great-grandparents. I know very few details about their daily lives or even our family history. Our family doesn't own any large pieces of land, and there are very few material inheritances to be had from Fredericks of the past. However, I am intensely grateful and forever indebted as I trace my faith inheritance back to them, and that is the greatest gift and legacy I could have ever asked for. Their faithfulness to the gospel, earnest commitment to prayer, and steadfast leadership of our family have bestowed upon me—our family and our children—the treasure of knowing Jesus. I hope and pray, by God's grace, that our great-grandchildren will feel the same way about us.

When you fight for your marriage, you battle fiercely for the eternal well-being of your children. You fight for your grandchildren. It can be said that the wake of your marriage today extends hundreds of years into the future. I don't say this to scare you but to urge you to trust Jesus even more. The salvation of your children isn't in your control; only

Christ can call and capture their hearts. But through your marriage, you are called to diligently till the soil of their hearts and plant seeds of the gospel. The ways you love and pursue each other, foster affection for Christ, and pass down your heritage of faith are all gospel seeds being planted and watered in the fertile soil of your children's hearts.

Your marriage covenant is the gospel exemplified for your children to see and hear in ways they wouldn't otherwise understand. Their faith doesn't ultimately depend on you, but your marriage can put them face-to-face with a living, breathing example of the beauty and wonder of the gospel for the good of generations to come.

How God's Family Is Strengthened

God values earthly family because it has always been a vital component in establishing his heavenly family. He created and commissioned the first family unit when he commanded Adam and Eve to "be fruitful and multiply" (Gen. 1:28). They obeyed and civilization erupted.

Throughout Scripture, the promises of God are passed down through blood. The Old Testament is rife with genealogical accounts, each charting family lineage as an important record of God's providential fulfillment of his covenant promises. One's family line was viewed as a résumé of sorts, and as such it was strongly tied to one's identity. It was through the family of Abraham that God promised to make Israel a great nation, and it would be through the same family line that Jesus entered humanity to fulfill the promise of redemption. Jesus's life, death, and resurrection sprung wide the doors of God's family to all who would place their trust in Christ. Today, the global church is God's family—we are his adopted children and coheirs with Christ (Rom. 8:17).

It is not surprising, then, that families anchored by the covenant of marriage are vital to bolstering and beautifying the local church. In the same way Asaph reminded fathers to teach their children "so that they should set their hope in God" (Ps. 78:7), Paul exhorted fathers in the Ephesian church to "bring [children] up in the discipline and instruction of the Lord" (Eph. 6:4). These charges and others like them are not just advice to parents for managing their children's behavior. They're divine calls to pass down the heritage of faith from generation to generation—and to multiply God's people, the church.

Communities Are Reached

As people who follow Jesus, you're adopted into the grace and love—the family—of God. You are his dearly loved and cherished children. Knowing and being known by God bear real fruit in your lives in the forms of love, joy, peace, and so much more (Gal. 5:22–23). These benefits are your birthright as adopted children of God. But God doesn't stop there.

Just as you're adopted into the family of God, you're commissioned to participate in his divine handiwork. He is your head; you are limbs of the body. "The church . . . is his body, the fullness of him who fills all in all" (Eph. 1:22–23). You are Christ's hands and feet in your community and, by extension of the global body of believers, the world. As marriages honor God, households are strengthened in Christ and the global body of believers is equipped to love and serve others, preach the gospel, and facilitate missional justice.

With this grander perspective we see the full magnitude of marriage *finally* taking form. You are called to a high calling of loving God and loving people, and your marriage is an avenue to sanctify you personally and to strengthen the action of the church globally.

How much more profound can the meaning of marriage be? Embracing the high calling of your marriage will anchor you in the never-ending and utterly meaningful purposes of God. Suddenly every struggle, every victory, and every mundane moment takes on new, profound meaning.

Selena and I pray that you and your spouse embrace God's sovereign design and purpose for your marriage and *fiercely* hold fast to Christ. We pray that you operate as one from a place of strength in Christ. And we pray that your affection for Jesus pushes you outward and you find yourselves witnessing and participating in Christ's work—as a couple and as a family—in ways you may have never imagined.

When we surrender our lives to Jesus we are ministers of his gospel. You need not be a vocational pastor or licensed priest (though that may be your calling). All followers of Jesus are his lay ministers (*lay* comes from *laity*, which means common people). Ministry is a byproduct of knowing God intimately and allowing him to pour out through us. In the same way, ministering through your marriage is an inevitable outcome of a loving covenant anchored in Christ.

Upward and Outward

We long to see Christian married couples *en masse* minister within and through *fierce* marriages. We aren't called to simply love each other fully and end our mission there. Let's explore our callings and live to see Christ change our world through the work he does in our marriages!

Marriages are the foundation of familial flourishing, families are the building blocks of the global church, and the church is God's ultimate Bride and plan A for reaching a world full of people who desperately need him.

Marriage is astoundingly allegorical. Everything about it points to the loving courtship between God and his people through the person and work of Jesus. We've come from perfection in the garden and we'll be made perfect again when united with Christ as his Bride. Until then, the sanctifying hand of God is hard at work preparing us for eternity, and covenant marriage is perhaps the tool he wields most.

Can you see it? Marriage is so much bigger than you! Thank God for that. Its purpose is far grander than just your love for each other. The covenant love your marriage embodies is a neon sign pointing us to the covenant promises of our powerful, loving, eternal God. Marriage is and always has been all about Jesus. A fierce marriage is all about God's endless love for you, his careful molding of your heart, and his unquenchable passion to reach the lost.

FOR REFLECTION

- How does it make you feel to know that Christ is fighting for your marriage?
- Do you see the larger purpose God has for your marriage? What is that larger purpose?
- In what areas do you see God using your marriage to advance his kingdom?
- What excites you most when thinking about how God can use you?

Acknowledgments

Having only our names on the cover feels misleading. We may have typed the enclosed words and sentences, but none of them would exist without the help of so many. A hearty thank-you is in order:

To Jeff and Alise for being our safe place when we needed it most. We are not the same because of you.

To Nathan and Anna for your friendship, enthusiasm, and laughter.

To Chad and Julie for your relentless support, encouragement, hospitality, and help.

To our early reviewers and theology-correctors: Rob, Kyle, Ron, Jake, Luke, Steven, and, of course, Dion. You kept us on the rails.

To Kerrie and Kyle; you showed us how to love people right where they are.

To Shawn; you caught the vision before anyone else and spurred it along. Let's hike again soon.

To the Monday night ladies; thank you for your support, ears, and hearts. Dion, Christie, Katie N., Katie B., Cari, Beth, Heather, Lisa, and Rachel, you are irreplaceable.

To Shannon, Justin, Katie, Cari, Kyla, Patrick, and the rest of the Vilicus team. Your faithfulness and diligence make things work with grace and poise. Each one of you is a gift from God.

To Bryan, the best literary agent in the entire galaxy and probably the universe. (Probably.)

To the entire Baker team for your investment in the kingdom and in this project. You helped us finally become authors.

To our parents; you watched the girls so we could sleep, think, write, stare at the screen, reconnect, go on dates, and recoup. Your help, prayers, and sacrifice are unprecedented and we love you!

To Grandpa Gordy; we wish you could have held a physical copy of this book in your hands, but Jesus had other plans. Thank you for your legacy of faith; we're eternally grateful.

Finally, to our sweet girls, Adelaide and Clementine. You didn't help much but we hope this book helps you whenever you get married (a very, very, very long time from now).

Thank you all; this book wouldn't exist without you. We wish there was a way to put all your names on the cover next to ours. Hopefully this page will suffice.

Much love,

Ryan and Selena

The Biblical Covenants

In chapter 3 we mentioned the many covenants in the Bible but didn't go into detail about them. However, Selena and I have found that it has greatly enriched, deepened, and bolstered our own marriage covenant to see it in the context of the unfolding covenants God has made with his people. Taking a grand view of God's covenantal action reveals much of his character and desire for marriage. We hope that our brief unpacking of the major biblical covenants below will encourage and challenge you as it does us.

God's Covenant with Adam

The Bible opens and immediately Jesus is actively involved. He was present for the creation of the world and of humankind: "Let us make man in *our* image, after *our* likeness" (Gen. 1:26, emphasis added). John 1:1–2 says, "In the beginning was the Word, and the Word was with God, and the Word was God. He was in the beginning with God." Christ, of course, is the Word.

Shortly after the creation account, God establishes his first covenant with Adam, humanity's representative:

> And the LORD God commanded the man, saying, "You may surely eat of every tree of the garden, but of the tree of the knowledge of good and evil you shall not eat, for in the day that you eat of it you shall surely die. (Gen. 2:16–17)

Adam is given access to everything the garden has to offer with one condition: don't eat from the tree of the knowledge of good and evil. The theological term for this short exchange is the Edenic Covenant. It's a conditional promise. Adam will remain in perfect relationship with God and flourish forever as long as he never eats of the tree. If he does, he will die a physical death as well as a spiritual one. In verses immediately following, God decides that Adam needs a helper, so he creates Eve.

Woman is created from man—flesh is separated by way of removing a rib—and the two are immediately joined back together as one through covenantal bond. From one, God made two unique image bearers of himself: man and woman. They were at once separate and distinct parts, two entirely different views of the same full image of God. They are then joined together in marriage.

From that point in Genesis, we begin to see language shift toward "her husband" and "his wife." The foundation is laid and the first marriage is complete.

This first wedding between Adam and Eve established the framework for the multiplication of humankind. God's first directive is clear: "Be fruitful and multiply and fill the earth and subdue it" (1:28). It established the unique partnership between one man and one woman, together foreshadowing a greater covenant between Christ and his Bride. Through this partnership, Adam and Eve were instructed to be fruitful and multiply. The marital union is at the absolute center of family and procreation. Within marriage, children are conceived and families flourish.

God's larger story continued. As you likely know, Adam and Eve broke the covenant with God by eating of the tree. They were ejected from the garden, and their perfect relationship with God was severed by sin. By God's grace, they were able to live on and "be fruitful and multiply," but outside the garden. Their original sin stained every generation from that point forward.

As a result of the fall, God made another covenant with Adam and Eve called the Adamic Covenant. God announced that there would forever be enmity between Satan, Eve, and her children (humankind). Eve would experience pain in childbirth, Adam would labor and toil as the land was cursed with thorn and thistle. There would be a distortion of roles and disunity in marriage: "Your desire shall be contrary to your husband, but he shall rule over you" (3:16). Finally, death would now be the inevitable end of all living things. However, even amid the curses because of their sin, God provided what many call the "First Gospel"—a promise that Satan (and death) would ultimately be defeated by one of Eve's offspring. This Redeemer from Eve's "seed" would be injured in the process of conquering Satan but arise triumphant (v. 15). Of course, the promised victor is Jesus Christ himself, and his injury, the cross.

God's Covenant with Noah

Generations after Adam and Eve, the world was in chaos. Sin had corrupted all of humanity to its core: "every intention of the thoughts of his heart was only evil continually" (6:5). God hit the reset button and flooded the earth. Before doing so, God found Noah "blameless in his generation" (v. 9) and chose to establish—or continue—his covenant through him. God didn't forget his earlier promise to Adam, and Noah (a direct descendent of Eve) would be a vital part of fulfilling it. You know the rest of the story: Noah built an ark, God flooded the earth, the waters receded, and Noah stepped onto dry land with his family after a year in the ark. After Noah gave a burnt offering, God made another promise called the Noahic Covenant. This time, God promised to never again flood the earth and destroy all life: "I have set my bow in the cloud, and it shall be a sign of the covenant between me and the earth" (9:13).

We often picture a rainbow overhead while Noah and his family hold each other affectionately and look up at it against the stormy sky. Yet the sign of the rainbow is so much more than a pretty image: it's a symbol of the grace of God and a foretelling of the gospel. With the storm set behind, God's bow—a symbol of war[1]—is pointed upward. Never again would people be the object of God's blanket wrath. Instead, he himself would bear the weight of sin and the total burden of salvation. Again, through covenant, God reminds us of his plan to redeem and save humankind through Jesus.

Are you getting a sense of how foundational these covenants are to the entire story the Bible tells? Stick with us; there's more.

God's Covenant with Abraham

Some centuries later, Abraham entered the scene and God made another covenant with him. This is called the Abrahamic Covenant, and it consists of three promises: God would give Abraham many descendants, he would give them land (Canaan), and from Abraham's descendants, humankind would be redeemed (12:1–3). As in the covenant with Noah, God alone bore the full weight of its requirements and reassured his people that a Redeemer was coming.

Abraham's family grew despite his sin and disbelief, because God kept his word. After a wild series of events, Abraham's grandson Jacob had twelve sons, including one named Joseph. He made his brothers jealous (because Jacob favored him), so they sold him to a caravan of Ishmaelites who took him to Egypt. Still, God is sovereign. Because of his God-given ability to interpret dreams, Joseph gained influence among Egyptian leadership. When famine hit Canaan, his brothers traveled to Egypt for help. There Joseph (in dramatic fashion) revealed his identity to them and appealed to Pharaoh to give them land in Egypt. Pharaoh obliged.

Abraham's family was displaced, but Joseph saw God working. He trusted that God would keep his promise by returning the family to Canaan one day: "As for you, you meant evil against me, but God meant it for good, to bring it about that many people should be kept alive, as they are today. . . . God will visit you and bring you up out of this land to the land that he swore to Abraham" (50:20, 24).

Even against all odds or convenience, God kept his promises and showed his trustworthiness through covenant. Abraham's descendants were many, their home was sure, and a

Savior would one day arrive to deliver God's people from death once and for all.

The covenantal theme continues.

God's Covenant through Moses

When Jacob (now named Israel) and his family moved to Egypt, there were seventy persons in total. They had yet to become the "great nation" God had promised they would be. The family, now called Israelites, remained in Egypt for several centuries, where they "multiplied and grew exceedingly strong, so that the land was filled with them" (Exod. 1:7).

Eventually a new pharaoh took the throne and he saw the Israelites as a threat. He oppressed them by enslaving them and mandating that every male Hebrew baby be thrown into the Nile. One of those babies was named Moses. Through the bravery of his mother and sister, Moses survived Pharaoh's mandate and became the adopted son of Pharaoh's daughter.

After many years and another wild series of events, God used Moses to free the Israelites from their harsh slavery. Just as he promised, Abraham would become a great nation:

> I will take you to be my people, and I will be your God, and you shall know that I am the LORD your God, who has brought you out from under the burdens of the Egyptians. I will bring you into the land that I swore to give to Abraham, to Isaac, and to Jacob. I will give it to you for a possession. I am the LORD. (6:7–8)

Once delivered from slavery in Egypt, the Israelites were battered and facing an empty, lifeless desert. Their bodies were weak and their faith weaker, but God's promise to his people was unchanged. He faithfully led them with a pillar of cloud by day and a pillar of fire by night. The Israelites were prone to doubt. Despite witnessing their own miraculous delivery from slavery, they constantly questioned God's plan. They longed for "simpler" times, when food was bountiful and life was relatively comfortable. They constantly forgot God's promise of a greater blessing: the land given to Abraham.

Amid their lack of faith, God established yet another covenant with his people. This time it was different. This time it was conditional. While God promised to bless them abundantly, it required something in return: obedience to God's law. This agreement is called the Old Covenant, or the Mosaic Covenant, and it began when Moses went to Mt. Sinai to receive the Ten Commandments. Its purpose was to govern Israel's behavior in order to maximize their trust in God and ensure that they would flourish. As long as they obeyed the law faithfully, God blessed them. If the people rebelled, God punished them.

While the Mosaic Covenant and its accompanying laws (outlined in the Mosaic and Levitical laws) were works-based, they didn't supersede God's earlier grace-based covenants. God's unconditional promises remained intact. Though his people repeatedly rebelled and lost faith, God never wavered in his desire, ability, or intention to fulfill the covenants he made: his people would still become a great nation, they would enter the promised land, and the Redeemer would still deliver them from death caused by sin in the garden.

After they had spent forty years of wandering the desert, Joshua finally led the Israelites into Canaan—a "land flowing with milk and honey"—just as God promised. Given

Israel's tendency to forget God's law and lordship, the book of Joshua opens with a stark reminder to avoid just that:

> Only be strong and very courageous, being careful to do according to all the law that Moses my servant commanded you. Do not turn from it to the right hand or to the left, that you may have good success wherever you go. (Josh. 1:7)

Now in their inherited land, the Israelites could finally put down roots and thrive. God's faithfulness had carried them through the desert and sustained them every step along the way. God did what he swore to do despite the countless times they turned away from him. Just before Joshua's death, he reminded the people to hold up their end of the promise. He compelled them to "fear the LORD and serve him in sincerity and faithfulness" (24:14).

To this, the people responded:

> Far be it from us that we should forsake the LORD to serve other gods, for it is the LORD our God who brought us and our fathers up from the land of Egypt, out of the house of slavery, and who did those great signs in our sight and preserved us in all the way that we went, and among all the peoples through whom we passed. . . . Therefore we also will serve the LORD, for he is our God. (vv. 16–18)

Thus, the people of Israel renewed their covenant with God and served him "all the days of Joshua, and all the days of the elders who outlived Joshua and had known all the work that the LORD did for Israel" (v. 31). It was a much needed time of rest, peace, and close relationship with God.

Do you see how much like a marriage God's relationship with Israel was? Do you see how these covenants are woven into the Bible's story and how important they are to God? That's how important your marriage covenant is.

We have another covenant to look at next.

God's Covenant with David

It didn't take long before Israel's faith began to slip. They "forgot the LORD their God and served the Baals and the Asheroth" (Judg. 3:7) and "everyone did what was right in his own eyes" (17:6), which is Bible-speak for rebellion against God's law. They broke their word and forgot their covenant; God's wrath was due.

This began a dark chapter in the story of God's people. In a few generations, they went from a time of rest and peace to a season rife with war and foreign oppression. Reading through Judges, we can see the pattern is cringe worthy: turn from God and suffer through punishment (usually by outsiders invading and raiding), turn back to God and cry out for deliverance, get delivered, repeat. The rebel-and-repent pattern continued for over three hundred years.

The people eventually begged for a king, so God appointed Saul. Many more wild events unfolded, Saul went sideways, and David was anointed as king. He, the youngest of all his brothers, was plucked from Bethlehem and chosen to be the new earthly king Israel desperately needed. He would help redeem his countrymen just as, one day, the ultimate Redeemer would rescue God's children. David was called a man after God's own heart, one who would do all his will (Acts 13:22). He was far from perfect, but God graciously made another covenant with him.

231

This new promise, dubbed the Davidic Covenant, was similar to God's covenant with Abraham. First, it was unconditional, and second, it reaffirmed redemption for God's people through the line of David (a descendant of Abraham):

> When your days are fulfilled to walk with your fathers, I will raise up your offspring after you, one of your own sons, and I will establish his kingdom. He shall build a house for me, and I will establish his throne forever. (1 Chron. 17:11–12)

In hearing God's promise, David erupted with worship! He said,

> There is none like you, O LORD, and there is no God besides you, according to all that we have heard with our ears. And who is like your people Israel, the one nation on earth whom God went to redeem to be his people, making for yourself a name for great and awesome things, in driving out nations before your people whom you redeemed from Egypt? And you made your people Israel to be your people forever, and you, O LORD, became their God. (vv. 20–22)

David had already experienced firsthand the faithfulness of God and the trustworthiness of his Word. As a kid, he had slain Goliath with nothing more than a rock and a prayer! David understood more than anyone the power of being in covenant with the Almighty, and he was overjoyed. His position with God was secure, and he knew nothing would ever change that.

The New Covenant through Christ

Fast-forward a few centuries; enter a baby. In the tiny town of Bethlehem, just as promised, our Redeemer—Jesus Christ—

was born. He lived the perfect life we couldn't live and died the gruesome death we should have died to pay the price for our sin and forever reconcile us to God. Just as blood sacrifices were required to atone for sin under the Old Covenant, Christ's blood is the only sacrifice sufficient to cover the sin of humanity for all time.

Jesus himself is the final promise—the New Covenant—that God made to his people. The birth, life, death, and resurrection of Jesus Christ brought us into the unprecedented period of grace we currently enjoy. By God's grace we have seen the repeated promises of a Redeemer fulfilled in the gospel. We can experience the immense joy David felt that day; when we are in Christ, God's love is unconditional, inexhaustible, and unwavering—it will never change. Jesus Christ—the "Son of David"—is on his throne forever, and the house he built is within the hearts of all believers through the gift and indwelling of the Holy Spirit.

God's faithfulness is clear, as evidenced through his various covenants with his people. It is God's nature to keep his word, the crescendo of which is in Christ—the Living Word of God.

The Culmination of God's Covenant

The end of the Bible climaxes with an eternal, perfect union of Christ and his Bride, where "he will wipe away every tear from their eyes" (Rev. 21:4). At this moment, the full New Covenant promised in Christ will at last be fulfilled. The same verse continues, "death shall be no more, neither shall there be mourning, nor crying, nor pain anymore."

The story concludes as the ultimate protagonists—the Bride (the church, believers) and the Lamb (Jesus)—are united in one final wedding. In this ultimate union all will be made new, there will be eternal celebration, and we will be finally united with our Bridegroom. Certainly, if there are tears at this wedding they will be tears of joy! "Come, I will show you the Bride, the wife of the Lamb" (v. 9).

Just as the first of God's people are sealed with covenantal promises, our final union with Christ is called a marriage. Throughout history and into eternity, God operates through covenantal promise. He proves his love to us by giving his Word and keeping it, many times, despite the rebellion of his people.

This type of love is impossible for us to grasp. It's *too* sacrificial, *too* relentless, *too* unconditional. We will never know love as God knows love—at least, not on this side of eternity. Maybe we'd obey perfectly if we did, but we don't. We're a fallen, sinful, and rebellious people prone to pride. Like the Israelites, we quickly forget the promises God made to us and his faithfulness in keeping them. We can witness his miracles and still grow doubtful. We are thick in the head and fast in the feet, hard of hearing and quick to seek other gods. That will always be the case until we are fully redeemed in Christ through glorious union with him. Until then, we have lots to learn about God's covenantal love and sufficiency.

That's the primary reason God structures marriage as a covenant. Your marriage is designed to help you more meaningfully understand the covenantal promises and unconditional love of God. Your difficulty in marriage and struggles with sin and forgiveness are redeemed within marriage to bring you closer to him. And marriage is one of God's major tools for teaching you the true depths of his unending love, forgiveness, mercy, and grace.

Notes

Chapter 2 Matters of the Heart

1. John Piper, "The Gospel in 6 Minutes," *Desiring God*, September 12, 2007, http://www.desiringgod.org/articles/the-gospel-in-6-minutes.
2. Gary Thomas, *Sacred Marriage* (Grand Rapids: Zondervan, 2000), 13.
3. C. S. Lewis, *Mere Christianity* (New York: Macmillan, 1952), 190.

Chapter 4 Gritty Love

1. "What Is Love? 0-100," YouTube video, 4:39, posted by SoulPancake, July 10, 2015, https://www.youtube.com/watch?v=_UWGKzqMwso.
2. Robert Sternberg, "A Duplex Theory of Love," in *The New Psychology of Love*, ed. Robert Sternberg and Karin Weis (New Haven, CT: Yale University Press, 2006), 184–99.
3. Euripides, "Iphigenia in Tauris," in *The Complete Greek Drama*, ed. Whitney J. Oates and Eugene O'Neill Jr., trans. Robert Potter (New York: Random House, 1938), http://www.perseus.tufts.edu/hopper/text?doc=Eur.%20IT%20275&lang=original.

Chapter 5 Time and Priorities

1. We got this idea to read, sing, and pray from Donald S. Whitney, *Family Worship* (Wheaton, IL: Crossway, 2016).

Chapter 6 Communication and Connection

1. C. S. Lewis, *The Four Loves* (New York: Harcourt, Brace, 1960), 89.

Chapter 8 Intimacy and Sex

1. Timothy J. Keller, "The Gospel and Sex," *Gospel in Life*, April 27, 2010, http://www.gospelinlife.com/the-gospel-and-sex.

Chapter 9 Dealing with Discord

1. As quoted in Thomas A. Tarrants III, "What God Wants from You," *Knowing and Doing* (Winter 2013), http://www.cslewisinstitute.org/What_God_Wants_from_You_FullArticle.

2. John Piper, "You Are Not Your Own: Romans 8:9," *Desiring God*, November 11, 2014, http://www.desiringgod.org/labs/you-are-not-your-own.

3. Timothy Keller with Kathy Keller, *The Meaning of Marriage* (New York: Riverhead, 2001), 278.

Chapter 10 Upward and Outward

1. Pew Research Center, "Parenting in America: Outlook, Worries, Aspirations Are Strongly Linked to Financial Situation," December 17, 2015, http://www.pewsocialtrends.org/files/2015/12/2015-12-17_parenting-in-america_FINAL.pdf.

The Biblical Covenants

1. The Hebrew word used for bow in Genesis 9:13, *qesheth*, is directly translated as "war bow." See https://www.blueletterbible.org/lang/lexicon/lexicon.cfm?Strongs=H7198&t=ESV.

Ryan and Selena Frederick created FierceMarriage.com in 2013 when they felt God calling them to share, with brutal transparency, the struggles he had helped them overcome. Since then, FierceMarriage.com has grown into a thriving online community with more than 200,000 unique visitors each month who generate more than 1,000,000 page views. Their social media presence is vibrant and growing, with more than 437,000 active fans and followers. Ryan also owns and manages emg, a marketing and web development company specializing in book launch marketing and programming. Ryan and Selena have two daughters and live in Tacoma, Washington.

CONNECT WITH
RYAN AND SELENA!

MORE FROM
FIERCE MARRIAGE

The 31 Day Pursuit Challenge Bundle offers a gospel-centered, practical path toward loving your spouse well.
Will you take the challenge?

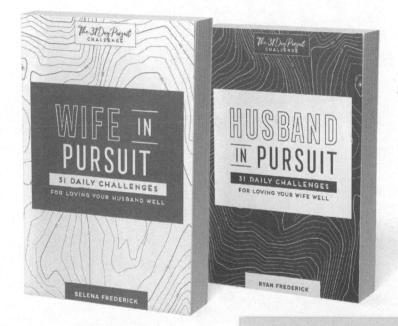

Draw closer to God and your spouse through 30 daily devotions, each one brought to life with imagery and practical application.

★ ★ ★ ★ ★

LIKE THIS
BOOK?
Consider sharing
it with others!

- Share or mention the book on your social media platforms. Use the hashtag **#FierceMarriage**.

- Write a book review on your blog or on a retailer site.

- Pick up a copy for friends, family, or strangers— anyone who you think would enjoy and be challenged by its message!

- Share this message on Twitter or Facebook: **I loved #FierceMarriage by @FierceMarriage**

- Recommend this book for your church, workplace, book club, or class.

- Follow Baker Books on social media and tell us what you like.

 Facebook.com/ReadBakerBooks

 @ReadBakerBooks